DEPOSITIONS:

PROCEDURE, STRATEGY AND TECHNIQUE

By

PAUL MICHAEL LISNEK, J.D., Ph.D.
Assistant Dean and Professor of Law,
Loyola University of Chicago School of Law

and

MICHAEL J. KAUFMAN, J.D.
Assistant Professor of Law,
Loyola University of Chicago School of Law

LAW SCHOOL AND CLE EDITION

ST. PAUL, MINN.
WEST PUBLISHING CO.
1990

COPYRIGHT © 1990 By WEST PUBLISHING CO.
610 Opperman Drive
P.O. Box 64526
St. Paul, MN 55164–0526

Library of Congress Cataloging-in-Publication Data

Lisnek, Paul M., 1958—
    Depositions: procedure, strategy, and techniques / by Paul M.
Lisnek, and Michael J. Kaufman.
        p.   cm.
    ISBN 0–314–73923–8
    1. Depositions—United States. I. Kaufman, Michael J., 1958-   .
II. Title.
KF8900.L57 1989
347.73'72—dc20
[347.30772]   89–27265
                                                       CIP

Lisnek & Kaufman
3rd Reprint—1993

PRINTED ON 10% POST
CONSUMER RECYCLED PAPER

DEDICATION

For my Parents—with love

PML

For my Family

MJK

*

ACKNOWLEDGEMENTS

———————

The road from concept to completion of a book is a notably long one for anyone who has chosen to travel it. These authors are grateful to several people who lightened the burden through their assistance to us.

The authors wish to thank in particular Judy Stevenson and the entire word processing staff at the law firm of Sachnoff & Weaver Ltd., without whose untiring assistance and support this book would not have been written. Deep gratitude is owed to Domini Graham Hunt, Esq. who assisted in researching the text from beginning to end. Although her initial work began as a third year law student, we are thankful that her devotion to the project remained until completion. We only hope the knowledge gained from the experience will be of benefit to her as she enters the exciting world of litigation. Providing hands-on experience and insight on the deposition process to Ms. Hunt were attorneys James M. Hoey, John F. Laughlin, Timothy J. McGonegle, and Orin S. Rotman whose efforts we appreciate.

It seems the more an author proofreads his text, the fewer mistakes he begins to see into the night. For their extensive assistance in this task, the authors thank Maureen T. McIntyre, Tisha M. Kelly and Kathryn Brett.

There were many days during the writing that administrative matters became notable interruptions to our work. Dean Lisnek extends heartfelt appreciation to his assistant, Michael H. Mendelson, for lending every possible support not just during this period but always. He is likely one of the finest administrators a law school could hope to employ.

Finally, but with utmost importance, we could not have undertaken (much less completed) this book without the unending cooperation and support of Loyola Law School Dean Nina S. Appel; her devotion to scholarship and faculty support is to be commended and respected.

P.M.L.
M.J.K.

*

PREFACE

We live in an increasingly litigious society. The lawyer carries a burden to limit and focus pretrial efforts expended so that the ultimate resolution of a case, be it settlement or trial, is reached only after following full case evaluation and preparation. It would be grave error indeed to experience an adverse verdict as a result of inherently damaging admissions or otherwise impeachable testimony which could have been prevented through effective deposition preparation. Trial lawyers need to fully supervise the preparation and investigation of every case through the pretrial stage; this book provides the planning mechanism for thorough preparation, execution and evaluation of depositions.

The deposition provides the discovery mechanism for gathering and probing information by which the examiner measures the plausibility and potential success of his or her intended trial position.

Yet, the deposition is, in a sense, a radical departure from the adversary system. This discovery device often requires a party to provide his adversary with all of the evidence which that adversary needs to win the lawsuit. It compels one party to share with the adversary evidence helpful to that adversary. As such, the attorney who presents his client for deposition is often in a no-win situation. The best that the presenting attorney can hope to achieve in the deposition is damage control. Because that paramount goal of damage control is pursued in an interaction which is self-policing, the presenting attorney has no immediate, external constraints on his tactics.

Supplementing the theoretical foundation from which the litigator prepares for deposition, this book provides a series of forms which enable the lawyer to apply directly the practical concepts to each case he or she is handling.

This book constitutes a step-by-step preparation guide assisting the attorney to decide which deposition to take or not take in each case. The attorney determines how each deposition can most effectively be taken, and how the information gathered from each deposition is to be integrated with the other pretrial mechanisms which comprise the discovery package. The outcome of any case is often hinged to the quality and depth of the depositions taken; it is well worth the attorney's time to both carefully read the concepts presented in this book and utilize those forms applicable in the attorney's own practice.

PAUL M. LISNEK
MICHAEL J. KAUFMAN

*

TABLE OF CONTENTS

PART I. PREPARING FOR THE DEPOSITION

TABLE OF CONTENTS

PART II. THE DEPOSING ATTORNEY'S PERSPECTIVE

PART III. THE DEFENDING PARTY'S PERSPECTIVE

TABLE OF CONTENTS

CHAPTER 14. USING THE DEPOSITION AT TRIAL—Continued

APPENDIX

Part I

PREPARING FOR THE DEPOSITION

Chapter 1

INITIAL QUESTIONS—PLANNING TO TAKE DEPOSITIONS

Table of Sections

---

§ 1.1 Deciding to Take the Deposition—The Factors

The decision to take a deposition requires evaluation of each potential deponent's knowledge of the case and his importance to the litigation; such decision is reached within the framework of purposes served by taking the deposition. While alternative discovery tools may uncover particular information, Form 1-1 permits attorneys to evaluate with ease the need for a deposition by reviewing all relevant considerations in a summary chart format.

Form 1-1 requires the attorney to specify the role each prospective deponent serves in the case vis-a-vis the relevant case issues and what that witness has to say or can prove with regard to each such issue. Beyond these considerations, the attorney also states why this information is needed through an importance rating scale. By evaluating the *alternative* means of obtaining that same information, the attorney can best decide whether each deposition should or should not be taken in the case.

Once completing Form 1-1's summary chart, the attorney considers the summary of the case issues en toto along with the importance ratings and indicates whether the deposition is one which must, should, is desirable to, should not or must not be taken. A section for comments and reasoning permits the attorney to memorialize the decision should he wonder at a later date whether such deposition was or is indeed necessary.

While attorney opinion may change regarding whether a deposition should be taken, it is important that the lawyers monitor their pretrial decisions through the litigation. Form 1–2 tracks the depositions taken as discovery proceeds, by providing a record of each party deposed, the name of the presenting attorney and relevant deposition information, including the court reporter service used and whether or not the transcript was ordered. A follow-up section requires the attorney to indicate the completion of transcript review, signature and filing. The latter part of the form monitors non-party witness addresses by requiring updating on a regular basis, thereby preventing loss of contact with non-party witnesses.

It is too often the case that a witness is unable to be located at the time of deposition or trial. As non-parties to the litigation, these witnesses cannot be expected to possess loyalty to the attorneys or the legal process; they may very well move their domicile without notifying anyone related to the litigation. If the non-party witness is not a close friend of or otherwise related to a party, it is unlikely that this person will be easily found. Indicating the source of the address information means a detective or other tracing service can better track down the witness should contact be lost.

§ 1.2 Advantages of Taking an Oral Deposition

Oftentimes, lawyers view depositions as an expensive discovery tool for which a better substitute should often be found. Nevertheless, several purposes are served by taking a deposition:

(1) An oral deposition may be taken 30 days after service without leave of court. Fed.R. Civ.P. 30(a).

(2) Before the commencement of an action, an oral deposition may be taken of any person with leave of court to perpetuate testimony.

(3) An oral deposition may be taken of parties and non-parties. Fed.R.Civ.P. 30(a).

(4) An oral deposition may be taken of a corporation, partnership, association or governmental agency, in which case the organization must designate an agent to testify on its behalf. Fed.R.Civ.P. 30(b)(6).

(5) Oral depositions are taken under oath. Fed.R.Civ.P. 30(c).

(6) The testimony taken at an oral deposition is recorded. Fed.R.Civ.P. 30(b)(4).

(7) The oral deposition of a party or its designated agent may be used by an adverse party for "any purpose." Fed.R.Civ.P. 32(a)(2).

(8) The oral deposition may be taken by telephone. Fed.R.Civ.P. 30(b)(7).

(9) An oral deposition may be videotaped. Fed.R.Civ.P. 30(c).

(10) Evidence taken at an oral deposition is generally received subject to objections. Fed. R.Civ.P. 30(c).

(11) A wide range of sanctions is available if the deponent fails to appear or cooperate in the deposition. Fed.R.Civ.P. 30(g); 37.

(12) Depositions enable an attorney to gather and probe information from opposing parties, witnesses, and anyone with knowledge directly or indirectly related to the case at bar.

(13) The information gathered and explored may be conducted over a period of a few hours, and not over the several weeks it might otherwise take to obtain answers to written interrogatories.

(14) The stagnant format of written interrogatory questions are no match for the spontaneous and flexible questioning or follow-up which deposition structure permits.

(15) Depositions enable the attorney to place limitations on and establish boundaries around the information disclosed by the deponent.

(16) The attorney can confirm the details of the deponent's story with previous statements made by or records of that deponent or other documents relating to that deponent's story.

(17) The adversary's story or position which runs contrary to your side can be identified through a deposition of either the adversary or a neutral deponent. These witnesses may possess damaging information which will highlight any weaknesses in the examining attorney's *own* case.

(18) The examiner can measure the demeanor for trial of potentially damaging witnesses.

(19) The appearance of one's *own* client and witnesses can be monitored.

(20) Testimony can be established to be used as admissions, for impeachment, or for other relevant evidentiary purposes at trial.

(21) Deposition preserves testimony of a witness not able to appear at trial because of age, illness, imprisonment, distance, death or other exceptional factors which prevent attendance. Where testimony will be supportive or of value, the attorney may anticipate one of these problems and proceed with the deposition.

(22) Testimony of witnesses, such as certain tightly-scheduled medical experts, can be recorded.

(23) Depositions narrow and clarify issues for trial.

(24) The examiner establishes credibility both with the deponent and other attorneys present, all of whom will be conducting a similar evaluation of their own.

(25) Testimony can be established to encourage settlement of the litigation.

(26) A relationship can be established with the deponent depending on the goals of the examiner. For example, an attorney may wish to create comraderie or adversity with the deponent as a means of posturing for subsequent settlement demands.

§ 1.3 Disadvantages of Taking an Oral Deposition

(1) The party taking the deposition must give reasonable notice of the deposition to the deponent and to every other party to the action. Fed.R.Civ.P. 30(b)(1).

(2) Where the witness is a non-party, a subpoena ad testificandum must be served in accordance with Federal Rule 45. Witness and mileage fees must accompany the subpoena.

(3) Because the oral deposition of a non-party may be taken only if a subpoena has been issued by the clerk of the district court where the deposition is to be taken, the deposing attorney must provide that clerk with a copy of the notice of deposition. Fed.R.Civ.P. 45(d).

(4) The oral deposition of a non-party witness must generally take place within 100 miles of where the witness works, transacts business or resides. Fed.R.Civ.P. 45(d)(2). Accordingly, attorneys must do the bulk of traveling to take a non-party's deposition.

(5) The deponent typically reserves the right to make changes in the deposition transcript before signing the transcript. Fed.R.Civ.P. 30(e).

(6) In practice, an oral deposition sometimes becomes an occasion for abusive tactics and attorney speechifying. The adversarial nature of the face-to-face confrontation and the absence of a neutral arbiter can combine to create an atmosphere of tension in which the attorneys "testify" more than do the clients.

(7) Some attorneys claim depositions are an expensive discovery tool. The expense of taking one, however, is more often outweighed by the considerable time and money spent both in executing written interrogatories and handling the numerous motions and hearings for compliance and sanctions held as a consequence.

(8) Depositions require a potentially unprepared adversary to review his file and ready himself for the deposition and, ultimately, trial. Assumed in this reasoning is the preparation of trial strategy and establishment of a settlement posture by the

adversary. However, a deposition taken early in the litigation, prior to investigation and study by the opponent, may produce helpful admissions.

(9) Depositions potentially place the examining attorney's trial strategy on the table and can alert the adversary to the existence of witnesses, thereby educating not only the deponent but the adversarial attorney. Of course, written discovery may similarly, albeit subtly, educate the opponent on case theory thereby shaping subsequent testimony.

The utility of the information obtained by the examiner will likely outweigh this often illusory disadvantage. The information received will be of greater value than the educating disclosure; the deposition will have been worth the effort. In a skillfully conducted deposition, the adverse party receives few helpful disclosures beyond a general awareness of the complexity of the litigation.

(10) Witnesses are rehearsed for trial through deposition, highlighting areas for improvement in both presentation and content of trial testimony. Much of the confidence gained is illusory since deposition testimony is taken in an attorney's office, outside the tension inherent in the courtroom environ.

(11) Depositions establish and preserve the testimony of the deponent which may necessitate modification in case strategy and presentation. Effective question design by the examiner, in which only information needed to pin down certain testimony is sought, can minimize the risk.

(12) Informal discovery may be an effective means for uncovering facts, but does not substitute for the deposition. While an attorney can speak with any non-party witness without notifying the opposing lawyer, it is improper to speak with an opposing party without the consent of his/her attorney (ABA Model Code of Professional Responsibility DR 7–104). Moreover, a non-party witness may deny at trial having made any previous statement.

(13) A deposition preserves testimony harmful to the lawyer's case which might otherwise have been unavailable at the time of trial. It is therefore advisable to evaluate and consider postponing the deposition of a witness expected to give harmful testimony.

After considering all of the disadvantages, there should be little doubt that deposition is the best tool available for pretrial discovery purposes. It permits the examining attorney to gather and probe information first-hand while simultaneously establishing the credibility of the deponent who will likely testify at trial. Such information is invaluable to effective trial preparation.

§ 1.4 Scope of Depositions

Determining the probative value and relevance of particular questions asked in depositions is often a difficult task since there is great variance in custom and practice among locations. Fed.R.Civ.P. 27 through 32 present the basic procedural framework within which deposition practice occurs. In reality, most problems which arise during depositions are resolved through cooperative attitudes and relationships between the attorneys. While there is no specific scope which defines deposition questions, there are boundaries beyond which attorneys will not permit a question to be posed. No judge is present to resolve disagreements, so the attorneys must exercise goodwill, guided by custom and practice, but modified by both their strategic motivation, and the nature of the relationship between the attorneys present. Maintaining good relations with fellow litigators, though they are often adversaries by definition, is more often recommended than not to produce peaceful resolution to disputes.

Fed.R.Civ.P. 29 specifically permits attorneys to take depositions in any mutually agreed upon manner; problems which cannot be resolved by the attorneys may be resolved through the judicial mechanism provided by Fed.R.Civ.P. 37. No substantial body of case law exists which would permit a directive resolution of many issues; judges necessarily turn to the governing practice and custom of the locale.

The rules governing deposition procedures extend to the determination of where the deposition will be held (Fed.R.Civ.P. 30(b)(1)). While plaintiffs and their agents are required to be available in the district where the action is pending, depositions of corporate officers or employees will usually be taken at the principal place of business. Special circumstances including hardship or financial burden on a particular party are factors which may lead a court to change the location of a deposition.

While the exact location of a deposition is often dependent upon attorney choice, the deposition is most commonly taken in the examining attorney's office. The deposition of a non-party witness, such as a medical expert, is often taken at that person's office; this strategy establishes good relations with the non-party witness, thus not antagonizing the witness.

Selecting the location of a deposition necessarily reflects the relationship intended to be established between the deponent and the examiner. While taking the deposition of a party at the party's attorney's office would provide the deponent with a familiar and comfortable surrounding, such an environ may or may not be desirable for the examiner, who usually notices the deposition at his/her own examiner's office. The examiner's office provides better control over the interaction and over interruptions.

§ 1.5   Organization of File Materials

The first step in formulating a deposition strategy is organization of the file. If the deposition occurs early in the life of the litigation the file may contain only a complaint and a notice of the deposition to be taken or defended; such posture presents few organizational problems. More likely, however, the file will be thick with a variety of materials. The file generally will contain: (1) pleadings (complaint, answer, amendments, motions, and legal memoranda supporting the motions), (2) prior discovery requests and prior discovery responses, (3) court orders, and (4) internal research and legal memoranda. Before a deposition takes place, these materials must be organized into a coherent structure which allows the attorney quick access to the desired information or documents.

Generally, when the attorney reaches for the file before a deposition, it already has some organizational form. A legal secretary or paralegal has separated the various parts of the file into neat subfiles with labels attached to each section. Every litigator knows that good legal secretaries and paralegals are life-savers. But in preparing for a deposition, mere reliance on even the best file organization is not sufficient. Rather, the attorney must start from square-one before each deposition.

First, the attorney must make sure that *all* relevant materials have made it to the file and that those materials are in the right place.

Second, the attorney must make sure that any documents in the file are marked or number-stamped and reorganized into a usable form.

Third, the attorney must ensure that an attorney or paralegal who "second-chairs" the deposition is as familiar with the file and its organization as the taking or defending attorney.

§ 1.6   Re-organizing the File for the Deposition

The attorney must *reorganize* copies of the file's pertinent materials into a form uniquely suited to the forthcoming deposition. This reorganization, which coincides with the attorney's development of a detailed substantive outline for each deposition should proceed as follows:

(1) Formulate a *substantive outline* which organizes the matters to be covered in the deposition into some discernible sequence: (a) by legal issues, (b) by time period, or (c) by contentions.

(2) Insert references to or quotations from the *pleadings* or relevant portions into each appropriate section of the substantive outline, particularly including:

(a) materials in the pleadings which may preclude attorney or witness from taking a contrary position at deposition or trial (i.e., allegations in the complaint); and

(b) materials in the adversary's pleadings which evidence admissions or possible positions to be taken at trial;

(c) materials in the adversary's pleadings which need not be established at the deposition because they have already been admitted;

(d) materials in the adversary's pleadings which can be used to impeach;

(3) Insert references to or quotes from the *discovery* responses or relevant portions into each appropriate section of the substantive outline, particularly including:

(a) interrogatory responses, documents or requests to admit which represent admissions by the attorney's deponent; and

(b) the adversary's interrogatory responses, documents or requests to admit which can be used to secure admissions or for impeachment.

(4) Insert into each appropriate section of the substantive outline the *proper legal standards,* gleaned from internal research and legal memoranda, which will enable the attorney to know what the deponent should or should not say with regard to each issue.

This method of file reorganization before each deposition has distinct advantages. Incorporating the pleadings and discovery responses into the substantive deposition outline, for example, allows the deposing attorney to know which admissions have already been made and need not be revisited. Often, questioning on admissions already made permits the party or witness to qualify those admissions. In addition, by re-organizing the pleadings and discovery responses in this way, the defending attorney can both better prepare the deponent and better defend the deposition against *material* admissions. Moreover, understanding particular buzz words in the case assists both the examining and defending attorneys to maintain the proper focus of mind. A defending attorney, who returns to the office after deposition believing that the adversary gained nothing, later realizes that a seemingly innocuous comment made by the deponent actually tracked the relevant legal standard, or that the adversary did not enter a crucial area only because an earlier admission rendered the inquiry unnecessary. Proper re-organization of the file for each deposition not only avoids these disastrous situations, but also places the attorney in control of the facts and the governing law.

§ 1.7 Tracking Non-deposition Discovery Materials

The attorney must monitor and compile all written discovery as completed prior to the deposition. It is not unusual for the busy litigator to find files in a state of disarray or confusion as pretrial discovery proceeds. Form 1–3 categorizes the written discovery taken and gathered prior to depositions, permitting the attorney to both better evaluate which depositions need be taken, and prioritize the order of depositions.

Form 1–3, Preparation for Deposition, organizes discovery by party and completion date. Separating the information gained from statements and interrogatories completed for each party, and evaluating the information disclosed from that discovery, places the attorney in a better posture to determine what further information is needed through deposition. The section on Form 1–3 relating to witnesses specifies whether that witness plays a fact or expert role, vis-a-vis his function in the litigation. The form enables convenient monitoring of the progress of written discovery and ensures that all necessary written discovery is completed prior to taking any depositions.

It is important that the attorney reviews *all* documentation gathered, not just interrogatories. Specifically, Form 1–5 enables the attorney to organize all documents by *type* of document for easy reference in deposition planning and in conjunction with the file organization system. Each document (statement, contract, lease or records) is set out with title, date, and summary being specified. The attorney sets out the key facts and comments on the importance of each such document for deposition planning.

Oftentimes, attorneys must locate a particular document which references needed information at a given moment. Together, Forms 1–3 and 1–4 enable the attorney to maintain knowledge of and control over both written discovery and produced documentation. Efficiency in deposition planning relies on easy access to documents.

§ 1.8 Organizing Documents for the Deposition

Once written discovery is properly organized in the file, Forms 1–6 and 1–7 assist the attorney to organize documents for use at each deposition.

Document to Deposition Preparation Form 1–5 requires the attorney to specify the name of each deponent, and all documents potentially relevant to that deposition. This form provides an easy means of locating documents when needed. Specifying the relevant information contained in each document vis-a-vis specific case issues enables the deposition to move along swiftly and with focus.

Document to Deposition Form 1–6 better details the document type as it relates to each case issue, relevant facts and citations. A section for commentary enables the attorney to specify strategy for using each document.

When combined, Forms 1–5 and 1–6 permit the attorney to master control over all documents as they relate to specific case issues. These forms are an important part of deposition preparation and efficient deposition execution. There is no reason an attorney should fumble for documents or facts under the pressure of the deposition.

The Issue Summary Chart (Form 1–7) requires the attorney to state each issue and his/her position with regard to it. The questions clarify the desired approach to each issue. The remaining categories seek corroborating, supplementing, contradicting and weakening facts, all of which are stated with regard to their source and file location. Specifying the deponent who can provide particular facts assists the examining attorney to gather and probe necessary information throughout all depositions.

§ 1.9 Understanding Each Side's Position

Each attorney creates a persona, or role, during the deposition which frames the atmosphere of the interaction. Each attorney uses those components of his/her personality which control the manner in which facts and emotions are conveyed. Like the actor on a stage, the attorney needs to present a logical and convincing persona to the other participants in the deposition.

Attorneys must maintain a high level of self-confidence, a thorough understanding of their own position, and clients of their opponent's position as well. This presentation develops within the limits of the attorney's own personality and realm of life experiences to hopefully produce a credible presence in the interaction. Practical skill development through continuing education programs is an imperative part of career development.

Form 1–8, Deposition Preparation: Understanding Position of Self, specifies each case issue and the attorney's position on the issue as well as opposing views. By specifying the corroborating, supplementing, contradicting and weakening facts set out on the Issue Summary Chart (Form 1–7), the attorney can utilize known facts to gain control over each particular issue.

Form 1–8 is to be used in conjunction with Form 1–9: Understanding the Position of Others. This latter form specifies each party's position in the litigation and allows the attorney to record and weigh the relative strength or weakness of the attorney's own position with opposing positions. The attorney specifies how he/she will deal with the opposing side's views by setting out the requisite steps which help the attorney carry out the clarified position (assuming a non-neutral position). Follow-up may include taking depositions of particular individuals, drafting interrogatories, requests to produce, requests to admit or conducting an inspection, all of which clarify necessary information to be gathered.

Form 1–10, the Attorney Self-Evaluation Sheet, monitors the attorney's record of performance in depositions and uncovers areas of relative strength and weakness regarding deposition preparation, analysis and attitude. Specifying the strengths of attorney character, as well as areas for improvement (in light of his/her existing reputation), will assist the attorney to establish a proper role in the interaction. Form 1–10 should be used in conjunction with Form 1–11, the Opposing Attorney Evaluation Sheet.

Form 1–11 goes beyond the information set out in the self-evaluation by requiring a short biographical sketch and personal prior history with the opposing attorney. This information and accompanying list of tactics employed by opposing attorneys enables the examining attorney to strategize on and establish an approach for each up-coming deposition. Form 1–11 also specifies desirable approaches and noteworthy cautions when working with or opposing another attorney, such background information being invaluable to establishing a proper posture in the deposition.

Forms 1–9 through 1–11 enable the attorney to achieve understanding of his/her position and the position of the opponent. Moreover, these forms enable the attorney to handle difficult attitudes and behaviors which may be presented in a deposition. The posture adopted by each attorney becomes a driving force in the development and monitoring of deposition interaction.

§ 1.10   Deposition Billing

Time is money; the efficient monitoring of time insures lower billing and a better return of client business. Forms 1–12 and 1–13 provide a means to monitor time expenditure while simultaneously establishing a billing record for each client. Clients appreciate specificity in attorney billing as well as efficiency in the handling of their case; these forms provide the requisite assurance desired by a client.

Form 1–12, the Billing Preparation Sheet, specifies the amount of time spent in preparation, at deposition and for deposition follow-up, respectively. The total time expended is specified on the form and subsequently transferred to the Time Billing Tracking Sheet (Form 1–13). This form compiles billing to indicate each deponent's name and role in the litigation along with the total time expended in preparation, at deposition and for summary follow through. The client is kept informed of each deposition and the element of surprise in billing is significantly reduced as the case progresses.

The forms intentionally do not include suggested billing rates or means of fee calculation, since rates vary significantly among attorneys. Attorneys should supplement Form 1–13 with their own billing rates while simultaneously monitoring overall case cost expenditure. Close monitoring of the case budget is the most important suggestion to offer an attorney who wishes to increase (not to mention maintain) case volume.

Form 1-1

Deposition Preparation—Deciding to Take a Deposition

Case _____ Client Name _____ File # _____

Prospective Deponent: _____

Role in Case: _____

Case Issue	What can witness prove?	Why information is important	Importance Rating	Alternative means to obtain info	Supplementary documentary proof needed
1.					
2.					
3.					
4.					
5.					

The above summary of case issues considered with facts proven and the issue importance rating leads me to conclude that this prospective deponent:

___ must ___ should ___ is desirable to ___ should not ___ must not be deposed.

Comments and Reasoning: _____

_____

_____

Date of last address confirmation: (To be updated every 6 months)

Source of Address: _____

___ Witness Report   ___ Telephone Directory   ___ Party Rpt

___ Dept of Motor Vehicles   ___ Other (Specify):

Corrected Address: _____

Correct as of: _____

Form 1-1

A. Name of Presenting Attorney: _____

    Law Firm Name: _____

    Firm Address: _____

    _____

    _____

    Firm Telephone: _____

B. Deposition Information:
    Date of Deposition: _____

    Court Reporter Service: _____

    Court Reporter: _____

    Court Reporter Telephone: _____

    Deposition ordered written? ___ Yes ___ No

    If yes, ordered by: _____

C. Transcript Receipt:
    Date Reviewed _____

    Date Signed _____

    Date Filed _____

Form 1–2

Deposition Record Form

Case _____ Client Name _____ File # _____

1. Name of party: _____

   ___ Plaintiff   ___ Defendant   ___ Third Party Def.

   A. Name of Presenting Attorney: _____

      Law Firm Name: _____

      Firm Address: _____

      _____

      _____

      Firm Telephone: _____

   B. Deposition Information:

      Date of Deposition: _____

      Court Reporter Service: _____

      Court Reporter: _____

      Court Reporter Telephone: _____

      Deposition ordered written? ___ Yes ___ No

      If yes, ordered by: _____

   C. Transcript Receipt:

      Date Reviewed _____

      Date Signed _____

      Date Filed _____

   2. Name of Witness:

      Favors: ___ Plaintiff   ___ Defendant

      Current Address: _____

      Address current as of: _____

Form 1–3

Preparation for Deposition

Case _____ Client Name _____ File # _____

1. Names of all Parties:

Plaintiff 1: _____

    Discovery Completed:

    1. Prior Statements:

        a. Date of Statement: _____

        b. Interviewer: _____

        c. Fact Summary: _____

           _____

           _____

           _____

    2. Interrogatories Completed:

        a. Propounded by: _____

        b. Date of Filing: _____

        c. Date Responses filed: _____

        d. Information Disclosed: _____

           _____

           _____

           _____

Plaintiff # 2: _____

    Discovery Completed:

    1. Prior Statements:

        a. Date of Statement: _____

        b. Interviewer: _____

c. Fact Summary: _____

_____

_____

_____

2. Interrogatories Completed:

a. Propounded by: _____

b. Date of Filing: _____

c. Date Responses filed: _____

d. Information Disclosed: _____

_____

_____

_____

Defendant # 1: _____

Discovery Completed:

1. Prior Statements:

a. Date of Statement: _____

b. Interviewer: _____

c. Fact Summary: _____

_____

_____

_____

2. Interrogatories Completed:

a. Propounded by: _____

b. Date of Filing: _____

c. Date Responses filed: _____

Form 1–3 (continued)

d. Information Disclosed: _____

_____

_____

_____

Defendant # 2: _____

Discovery Completed:

1. Prior Statements:

    a. Date of Statement: _____

    b. Interviewer: _____

    c. Fact Summary: _____

_____

_____

_____

2. Interrogatories Completed:

    a. Propounded by: _____

    b. Date of Filing: _____

    c. Date Responses filed: _____

    d. Information Disclosed: _____

_____

_____

_____

Defendant # 3: _____

Discovery Completed:

1. Prior Statements:

    a. Date of Statement: _____

    b. Interviewer: _____

Form 1-3 (continued)

c. Fact Summary: _____

_____

_____

_____

_____

2. Interrogatories Completed:

a. Propounded by: _____

b. Date of Filing: _____

c. Date Responses filed: _____

d. Information Disclosed: _____

_____

_____

_____

Third Party Defendant: _____

1. Prior Statements:

a. Date of Statement: _____

b. Interviewer: _____

c. Fact Summary: _____

_____

_____

_____

_____

2. Interrogatories Completed:

a. Propounded by: _____

b. Date of Filing: _____

c. Date Responses filed: _____

Form 1–3 (continued)

d. Information Disclosed: _____

_____

_____

_____

2. Names of all Witnesses:

a. Name: _____ Fact _____ Expert _____

Role in Case: _____

_____

_____

Discovery Completed:

1. Prior Statements:

    a. Date of Statement: _____

    b. Interviewer: _____

    c. Fact Summary: _____

_____

_____

    d. Witness Impression: _____

_____

_____

2. Interrogatories Completed:

    a. Propounded by: _____

    b. Date of Filing: _____

    c. Date Responses filed: _____

    d. Information Disclosed: _____

_____

_____

Form 1-3 (continued)

b. Name: _____

Discovery Completed:

1. Prior Statements:

    a. Date of Statement: _____

    b. Interviewer: _____

    c. Fact Summary: _____

        _____

        _____

    d. Witness Impression: _____

        _____

        _____

2. Interrogatories Completed:

    a. Propounded by: _____

    b. Date of Filing: _____

    c. Date Responses filed: _____

    d. Information Disclosed: _____

        _____

        _____

c. Name: _____

Discovery Completed:

1. Prior Statements:

    a. Date of Statement: _____

    b. Interviewer: _____

    c. Fact Summary: _____

        _____

        _____

     d. Witness Impression: _____

                 _____

                 _____

2. Interrogatories Completed:

     a. Propounded by: _____

     b. Date of Filing: _____

     c. Date Responses filed: _____

     d. Information Disclosed: _____

                 _____

                 _____

Document Organization Preparation Sheet

Case _____ Client Name _____ File # _____

Document Type   Statement

    Title   _____

    Date   _____

    Interviewer   _____

    Summary: _____

_____

_____

_____

    Key Facts: _____

_____

_____

_____

_____

    Comments: _____

_____

_____

_____

Document Type   Contract/Lease

    Title   _____

    Date   _____

    Interviewer   _____

    Summary: _____

_____

_____

_____

Key Facts: _____

_____

_____

_____

_____

Comments: _____

_____

_____

_____

Document Type   Records

Source: ___ Medical   ___ Accounting   ___ Police

     ___ Court   ___ Inspection   ___ Business

     ___ Employee   ___ Hearing Transcript

     ___ Other (Specify)

Title   _____

Date(s)   _____ to _____

Prepared by   _____

Summary: _____

_____

_____

_____

_____

_____

Key Facts: _____

_____

_____

_____

_____

Form 1–4 (continued)

Comments: _____

_____

_____

_____

_____

Form 1–5

Document To Deposition Preparation Form

Case _____ Client Name _____ File # _____

Deposition of: _____

Document Type	Title of Document	Specific Relevant Information	Page or Sec Cite
Statement			
Contract			
Record:Med			

Form 1–6

Document to Deposition

Case _____ Client Name _____ File # _____

Deposition of: _____

Document Type: _____

Specific Title: _____

	Issue	Fact	Citation	Comments
1.				
2.				
3.				
4.				
5.				

Issue Summary Chart

State Issue: _____

_____

_____

Your Position: _____

_____

_____

Corroborating Facts	Source	Cite	Necessary Deposition
Supplementary Facts	Source	Cite	Necessary Deposition
Contradictory Facts	Source	Cite	Necessary Deposition
Weakening Facts	Source	Cite	Necessary Deposition

Form 1–8

Deposition Preparation—Understanding Position of Self

Case _____ Client Name _____ File # _____

1. State issue: _____

   _____

   _____

2. State *your* position on the issue: _____

   _____

   _____

   _____

3. Clarify the opposing position(s) to the issue: _____

   _____

   _____

   _____

4. What known facts corroborate your position? _____

   _____

   _____

   _____

5. What known facts supplement your position? _____

   _____

   _____

   _____

6. What known facts contradict your position? _____

   _____

   _____

   _____

7. What known facts weaken your position? _____

   _____

   _____

   _____

Form 1-9

Deposition Preparation—Understanding the Position of Others

Case _____ Client Name _____ File #_____

Party Name (Other than self) _____

____ Plaintiff   ____ Defendant   ____ Third Party Def.

Party's position in the Litigation:

1. What facts support the position? _____

   _____

   _____

2. What facts weaken the position? _____

   _____

   _____

3. Your opinion regarding the other's position:

   ____ Agree   ____ Disagree   ____ Neutral

   ____ it's strong   ____ it's weak   ____ Unsure

4. Specify your desired response to the position:

   ____ Confirm it   ____ Attack it   ____ do not investigate

5. Steps necessary to carry out your position as specified in Questions 3 and 4: (assuming no neutral or "do not investigate" position is taken).

   a. Depose the following individuals: (specify role in case) _____

   _____

   _____

   _____

   b. Draft interrogatories to: _____

   _____

   specify issues for interrogatories: _____

   _____

c. Prepare Request for the following documents: _____

_____

d. Prepare Requests to admit as follows: _____

_____

e. Notice the following inspection: _____

_____

Form 1–10

Attorney Self Evaluation Sheet

1. Deposition Record

Case Name	Date	Deponent	Tactics Employed	Strong Moments	Weak Moments	Skills to Improve

2. Factor Strengths and Weaknesses

Factor	Strengths	Weaknesses
Preparation		
Legal analysis		
Attitude toward other lawyers		
Attitude toward client/witness		

3. Strengths of Personal Character: _____

_____

_____

4. Areas to Improve Character: (ego, involvment, relations) _____

_____

_____

5. Personal Reputation: (as reported by others)

Case Name	Date	Activity	Opinion	Facts

Opposing Attorney Evaluation Sheet

Attorney Name: _____

Current Firm: _____

Biographical Sketch: (education, work experience, special skills) _____

_____

_____

Prior Cases with you/your office: _____

Case Name	Settlement or Verdict Amount	Performance Rating

Reputation:

Role	Strengths	Facts	Weaknesses	Facts
opposing lawyer				
co-defendant				
co-plaintiff				

Factor	Strengths	Facts	Weaknesses	Facts
Legal analysis				
competency				
attitude to other lawyers				
attitude to witnesses/client preparedness				
credibility of opinion				

Tactics Employed:

Tactic	When employed	Against Whom (personality type)	Comments

Best approach to use when working *with* this attorney?

_____

_____

_____

Best approach to use when *opposing* this attorney?

_____

_____

_____

Cautions to note when *working with* this attorney:

_____

_____

_____

Cautions to note when *opposing* this attorney:

_____

_____

_____

Form 1–11 (continued)

Form 1–12

Billing Preparation Sheet

Case _____ Client Name _____ File #_____

1. Name of Deponent: _____

2. Preparation Time

    a.   Document Review   _____

    b.   Question Outline Preparation   _____

    c.   Witness Preparation Session   _____

3. Deposition Time

    a.   Start Time   _____

    b.   End Time   _____

4. Deposition Summary

    a.   Organization of notes   _____

    b.   Draft Fact Summary   _____

    c.   Draft Witness Impression   _____

    d.   Prepare plan for follow-up discovery   _____

       TOTAL TIME   _____

Time Billing Tracking Sheet

Case _____ Client Name _____ File #_____

Deponent Name & Case Role	Date Taken	Preparation Time	Deposition Time	Summary Time	Total Time
1.					
2.					
3.					
4.					
5.					

Chapter 2

THE TOOLS OF DISCOVERY

Table of Sections

---

§ 2.1 Alternatives to Oral Deposition

Five discovery methods exist as alternatives to an oral deposition:

(1) interrogatories;

(2) requests for the production of documents or other tangible material;

(3) physical or mental examinations;

(4) requests to admit; and

(5) written depositions. *See e.g.* Fed.R.Civ.P. 30–36.

Attorneys may employ any or all of these devices in a single case. Moreover, attorneys may use these discovery methods in any sequence. Accordingly, in developing a discovery strategy, attorneys should consider the advantages and disadvantages of each discovery device in light of their discovery objectives.

§ 2.2 Discovery Objectives

Discovery performs both a systemic and an adversarial function. Pre-trial discovery enables the system of adjudication to reduce the genuine issues of material fact which must be resolved at trial. Also, discovery helps the system to weed out claims that may have been well-pled, but which, after discovery, turn out to have no basis in fact. Finally, discovery may encourage the settlement of disputes.

For the adversary, discovery is used *inter alia*, to:

(1) gather evidence for proof at trial;

(2) preserve evidence not available at trial;

(3) produce admissions which can be used at trial or in settlement negotiations;

(4) uncover claims or defenses previously unconsidered;

(5) foster settlement negotiations generally;

(6) reveal the strengths and weaknesses of potential trial witnesses; and

(7) refine theories of the case.

With these goals in mind, the attorney should evaluate each of the discovery alternatives.

§ 2.3 Interrogatories—Advantages and Disadvantages

Interrogatories are a series of written questions served by a party upon another party. Each question must be answered "separately and fully in writing under oath, unless it is objected to, in which event the reasons for the objection shall be stated in lieu of an answer." Fed.R.Civ.P. 33(a).

Advantages

1. Interrogatories may be served without leave of court. Fed.R.Civ.P. 33(a).

2. They may be served upon a party contemporaneously with the filing of the complaint. Fed.R.Civ.P. 33(a).

3. They must be answered within 30 days, or 45 days if served with the complaint. Fed.R. Civ.P. 33(a).

4. They must be answered under oath. Fed.R.Civ.P. 33(a).

5. The answers must be signed by the responding party. Fed.R.Civ.P. 33(a).

6. The answers may be used at trial as admissions, or for impeachment. Fed.R.Civ.P. 33(b). Moreover, their use is not limited to the pending action. Gidlewski v. Bettcher Industries, Inc., 38 Fed.R.Serv.2d 664 (E.D.Pa.1983).

7. They may be served upon a corporate party, in which case they must be answered by an officer or agent who will furnish all information available to the party itself. Fed.R.Civ.P. 33(a).

8. They may seek an opinion or a contention of an adversary that relates to the application of law to fact. Fed.R.Civ.P. 33(b).

   (a) These so-called "contention interrogatories" permit a party to discover all of the facts or materials which support the contentions contained within its adversary's pleadings.

   (b) Contention interrogatories allow the relevation of trial strategies.

   (c) Contention interrogatories also furnish a basis for Fed.R.Civ.P. 11 sanctions if the answering party is unable to proffer any facts or materials which support the contentions in its pleadings.

9. Interrogatories may also be used without leave of court to obtain the identity of each expert whom a party expects to call as a trial witness, including the subject matter, substance and summary of the expert testimony. Fed.R.Civ.P. 26(b)(4)(A)(i).

10. Interrogatories, prepared by an attorney in his own office in a format typically contained in a word processing memory bank, tend to be less expensive than other forms of discovery.

Disadvantages

1. Interrogatories may not be served on non-parties.

2. Local rules limit the number of interrogatories which may be served. *See e.g.* Local Rule 9(g), Northern District of Illinois (June 20, 1975), limiting to 20 the number of interrogatories that any party may serve.

3. Interrogatories do not test the demeanor of the answering party.

4. Interrogatory responses cannot be immediately followed with additional, more probing, questions. Accordingly, interrogatories are ill-suited for detailed accounts of the facts which gave rise to the litigation.

5. Interrogatories need not be answered at all if the answer can be ascertained from the party's business records, in which case the party need only specify the relevant records. Fed.R.Civ.P. 33(c).

6. In practice, interrogatories are frequently evaded because they may be "objected to" in lieu of an answer. Interrogatories often result in a war of compliance. Answers, if they come at all, are typically late or incomplete.

7. The burden of seeking compliance is upon the interrogating party. That party must seek a court order under Fed.R.Civ.P. 37(a) compelling interrogatory responses.

§ 2.4 Use of Interrogatories

Interrogatories are best used to obtain general, background information about an adversary or an adversary's case. They are a cost-effective method of discovering valuable objective information such as the identities of lay and expert witnesses, the existence of documents, the status, corporate or otherwise, of the adversary, the employment or personnel structure of the adversary, financial data and the existence of any events or transactions related to the litigation-provoking event or transaction. Most attorneys feel that the utility of interrogatories relative to alternative discovery devices diminishes as the information sought becomes more detailed.

Interrogatories can also be used, however, in a strategic fashion. The contention interrogatory allows the interrogating attorney to obtain all of the facts supporting his adversary's allegations well in advance of trial. The absence of a sufficient response to a contention interrogatory raises the possibility that *no* facts support the adversary's allegations, in which case Fed.R.Civ.P. 11 sanctions may be proper. A sufficient response to the contention interrogatory, on the other hand, reveals a great deal about the opponent's case, locks that opponent into the totality of facts which the opponent, at that time, believes support his allegations and sets the stage for further discovery or settlement negotiations.

Moreover, interrogatory responses can be used tactically at trial as admissions. Although interrogatory responses can be, and often are, amended before trial, the fact that they have been amended itself has tremendous impeachment value. Forms 2–1 and 2–2 provide a method of cataloging the information received in response to interrogatories so that the information may be helpful at the deposition.

§ 2.5 Requests for Production—Advantages and Disadvantages

Any party may serve upon another party a request to produce, or to enter land to inspect, documents or tangible things in the possession, custody or control of the other party. Fed.R. Civ.P. 34(a). A party served with such a request must within 30 days, or 45 days if served with the complaint, permit the request for inspection, produce the documents as they are kept in the usual course of business or in an organized form or state a proper objection. Fed.R.Civ.P. 34(b).

Advantages

1. Requests to produce may be served without leave of court.   Fed.R.Civ.P. 34(a).

2. They may be served upon a party contemporaneously with the filing of the complaint. Fed.R.Civ.P. 34(b).

3. They must be responded to within 30 days, or 45 days if served with the complaint.   Fed.R. Civ.P. 34(b).

4. They result in the production of "real" evidence, rather than information or responses prepared for litigation.

5. They often result in the production of business records, which can be admitted into evidence under an exception to the hearsay rule.

6. Because the number of documents to be produced is often so great that the producing party does not have the time to pre-screen the documents, the discovering party may obtain "smoking guns" or privileged material.

7. Requests for production or inspection can be disruptive to an adversary, particularly where it is a small business.

Disadvantages

1. Discovery of documents and tangible things from non-parties is only permitted under Fed. R.Civ.P. 45(d) in connection with the taking of a deposition, or by way of an independent action.   Fed.R.Civ.P. 34(c).

2. Documents provide only circumstantial evidence; they rarely contain admissions.

3. Documents produced are typically pre-screened.

4. Numbering, organizing, categorizing and reviewing the documents produced can consume tremendous time and resources.

5. In practice, complete compliance with a request to produce documents routinely involves motions to compel production before a court or magistrate.

§ 2.6   Use of Requests to Produce

Documents rarely contain express statements by a party regarding issues at stake in the litigation; they do contain statements made by a party before the party has assumed a litigation posture.   Accordingly, they can reveal candid information.   Further, they can be pieced together to create a story or theory of the case.   Finally, document productions are an essential defensive device by permitting an attorney to be prepared for evidence that the adversary may introduce at trial.   Forms 2–3 and 2–4 provide a method of cataloging documents so that they may be used at the deposition.

§ 2.7   Physical and Mental Examinations—Advantages and Disadvantages

A party may move the court in which an action is pending to order another party to submit to a physical or mental examination.   Fed.R.Civ.P. 35.   The court may order such an examination only if the mental or physical condition of the party or its agent is in "controversy," and the requesting party has made an "affirmative showing" that "good cause" exists for the examination.   See Schlagenhauf v. Holder, 379 U.S. 104, 85 S.Ct. 234, 13 L.Ed.2d 152 (1964); Fed.R.Civ.P. 35.   Physical and mental examinations are unusual discovery devices which are available where they are the sole method of discovering information probative of an issue in genuine dispute.   An order granting such an exam will specify its time, place, manner and limited scope.   Fed.R.Civ.P. 35(a).

Advantages

1. A physical or mental exam allows one party to hire its own physician to examine the other party.

2. The exam produces strong evidence of the actual physical or mental condition of the adversary.

3. The very possibility of exam is a potent weapon in settlement negotiations.

4. If the examined party requests a copy of the physician's findings, the examining party may then receive a copy of any like report of any and all examinations performed on the examined party. Fed.R.Civ.P. 35(b).

Disadvantages

1. Physical or mental exams may not be taken of anyone except parties or their agents. Fed.R.Civ.P. 35(a).

2. The exams are only available with leave of court, upon a showing of "good cause." Fed.R.Civ.P. 35(a).

3. The scope of the information discovered is necessarily limited.

4. The results of the exam must be tendered to the adversary upon request.

§ 2.8 Use of Physical and Mental Examinations

These examinations are best employed in the narrow circumstance where the information cannot be obtained through any alternative discovery device. Indeed, "good cause" to take the exam requires some showing that the exam is necessary to obtain information which is probative of a genuine issue and which cannot be obtained elsewhere.

Apart from its fact-finding value, however, physical and mental exams have great tactical significance. The spectre of such an exam induces settlement. Moreover, in order to protect their clients from the ordeal of the exam, attorneys may remove from "controversy" an issue which had previously been "in controversy." Suppose, for example, that a defendant claims to have discharged the plaintiff because of a drinking problem and seeks a physical examination of the plaintiff to "prove" the drinking problem. The plaintiff's lawyer may decide to admit the plaintiff's drinking problem just to remove the issue from controversy and avoid the examination. The defendant thereby has gained an admission on an issue previously in controversy merely by raising the prospect of the exam. Forms 2-5 and 2-6 provide a method of cataloging the results of a physical or mental examination so that those results can be used at the deposition.

§ 2.9 Requests to Admit—Advantages and Disadvantages

A party may serve upon another party a request that the served party admit the truth of any matter written in the request, including opinions, facts, the application of law to fact or the genuineness of documents. Fed.R.Civ.P. 36. The written matters will be deemed admitted unless the served party denies the matters or objects to them within 30 days. Fed.R.Civ.P. 36.

Advantages

1. Requests to Admit may be served without leave of court. Fed.R.Civ.P. 36(a).

2. Requests to Admit may be served at any time during the litigation, including contemporaneously with the filing of the complaint. Fed.R.Civ.P. 36(a).

3. Requests to Admit contain a self-executing sanction; matters not denied or objected to within 30 days (45 days if served with the complaint) are deemed admitted. Fed.R.Civ.P. 36(a).

4. Matters admitted are "conclusively" established for trial unless the court upon motion permits the withdrawal or amendment of the admission. Fed.R.Civ.P. 36(b).

5. Requests to Admit may produce admissions regarding the application of law to fact. Fed.R.Civ.P. 36(a).

6. Requests to admit may produce admissions regarding the genuineness, and admissibility, of documents to be introduced into evidence at trial. Fed.R.Civ.P. 36(a).

7. Requests to Admit eliminate genuine issues of fact, thereby allowing the litigants to focus their efforts on matters still in controversy.

8. Although Requests to Admit require a great deal of thought, they do not consume tremendous time and resources. Nor do they require significant client time.

Disadvantages

1. Requests to Admit may not be served on nonparties. Fed.R.Civ.P. 36(a).

2. Admissions made by a party are binding only in the pending action and cannot be used for any other purpose or in any other proceeding. Fed.R.Civ.P. 36(b).

3. The responding party may in lieu of a response state that it is unable to admit or deny the matters, so long as the responding party sets forth in detail the reasons for its inability to do so or states that despite its reasonable inquiry it has insufficient information with which to admit or deny. Fed.R.Civ.P. 36(a).

4. Requests to Admit are rigid; they can produce admissions of stated matters, but they cannot be used to probe those matters in increasing detail.

5. Requests to Admit require the discovering party to have enough information about the case to be able to formulate matters which may be admitted. Accordingly, their use presumes prior discovery.

§ 2.10 Use of Requests to Admit

Although Requests to Admit can be served at the inception of litigation, they perform a pre-trial function. As trial approaches and alternative methods of discovery have been exhausted, the litigants will begin to develop their proof. Requests to Admit allow a party to eliminate matters on which proof will be necessary. If the requests are carefully if not subtly drafted, the admissions may provide the basis for a summary judgment motion. In addition, requests to admit the genuineness of documents can either eliminate evidentiary battles at trial, or forewarn litigants that they may need to call additional witnesses to ensure that exhibits will be admitted into evidence. Forms 2–7 and 2–8 provide a method of cataloging the responses to requests to admit so that these responses can be used at the deposition.

§ 2.11 Written Depositions—Advantages and Disadvantages

A party may take and record the testimony of any person by compelling the person to answer a series of written questions under oath. Fed.R.Civ.P. 31.

Advantages

1. After the commencement of any action, written depositions may be taken without leave of court. Fed.R.Civ.P. 31(a).

2. Before the commencement of an action, written depositions may be taken of any person with leave of court to perpetuate testimony. Fed.R.Civ.P. 27.

3. Written depositions may be taken of parties and non-parties. Fed.R.Civ.P. 31(a).

4. Written depositions may be taken of corporations, partnerships, associations or governmental agencies, in which case the organization must appoint a knowledgeable agent to respond to the questions. Fed.R.Civ.P. 31(a).

5. Although immediate follow-up questions are impossible, the rules do permit a series of follow-up, cross and re-direct questions. Fed.R.Civ.P. 31(a).

6. The written deposition of a party or its designated agent may be used by an adverse party for "any purpose." Fed.R.Civ.P. 32(a)(2).

7. The written deposition of a non-party may be used at trial for impeachment. Fed.R.Civ.P. 32(a)(1).

8. The written deposition of a non-party may be used for any purpose if the non-party is unavailable. Fed.R.Civ.P. 32(a)(3).

9. The written deposition requires careful drafting, but is relatively inexpensive.

Disadvantages
1. Written depositions do not test the demeanor of the witness.
2. Responses to written depositions cannot immediately be followed-up.
3. Written depositions do not allow the deposing attorney to clarify questions.

§ 2.12 Use of Written Depositions

Written depositions have six valuable uses. First, unlike interrogatories, written depositions can be taken of non-parties. Accordingly, they provide the functional equivalent of interrogatories for non-parties. Second, written depositions may be accompanied by a subpoena for documents under Fed.R.Civ.P. 45(d), in which case such documents can be discovered from a non-party. Third, written depositions provide a cost-effective alternative to oral depositions, particularly in smaller cases where the amounts in controversy may not warrant an expensive oral deposition of every witness. Fourth, written depositions allow the discovery of essential information from otherwise minor witnesses. Fifth, written depositions are useful to preserve the testimony of a witness who will not be available at trial. Finally, written depositions can be used to record the testimony of a friendly witness. Such a deposition is not only helpful at trial, but it may provide the basis for evidence supporting or opposing a summary judgment motion. Form 2–9 provides a method of cataloging the evidence received at a written deposition.

§ 2.13 Sequencing Discovery Devices—The Authority to Sequence

The "methods of discovery may be used in any sequence" unless the court, for the convenience of the parties and in the interests of justice, orders otherwise, Fed.R.Civ.P. 26(d). The discovery rules further allow the multiple use of each device. As a general rule, attorneys may freely craft a discovery plan or strategy which employs each of the devices in the most effective order.

Some limitations on this discovery freedom, however, should be kept in mind. First, discovery may not be taken *before* an action is commenced, except with leave of court to take a deposition to perpetuate testimony. Fed.R.Civ.P. 27. Second, if the plaintiff serves interrogatories, requests to produce or requests to admit with the complaint, the defendant is allotted 45 days, rather than the typical 30 days, to respond. Fed.R.Civ.P. 33, 34. Third, the court has discretion to shorten or enlarge the time for responding to interrogatories, requests to produce or requests to admit, and can exercise that discretion so as to allow defendants enough time to secure counsel before responding to discovery requests. *See* Fed.R.Civ.P. 33, 34, 36. Fourth, the court may on its own, or must upon motion, establish a plan and schedule of discovery which includes a discovery cut-off date. Fed.R.Civ.P. 26(f). Fifth, the court has authority pursuant to Fed.R.Civ.P. 26(c) to enter a protective order requiring that discovery be accomplished only at a certain time or by a certain method. Sixth, the district court has a duty in some cases to sequence discovery in a manner that will limit any burden on the responding party. *See e.g.,* Marrese v. American Academy of Orthopaedic Surgeons, 726 F.2d 1150 (7th Cir.1984). Finally, in ordering a physical or mental examination, the court will consider whether alternative methods of discovering the same information can be explored, thus obviating the need for the exam. *See* Fed.R.Civ.P. 35.

§ 2.14 Developing a Sequence—The Pyramid Approach

The most common method of sequencing discovery is the pyramid approach. Under this approach, each discovery device builds on previous more general requests so that the information sought and obtained becomes increasingly detailed and precise. Attorneys aim their discovery requests at specific information, the importance of which has been made clear by prior requests. The pyramid method also avoids unnecessary or duplicative discovery requests.

The following sequence is suggested by the pyramid method:

1. Interrogatories of a general nature served contemporaneously with the complaint or answer.

2. Requests for the production of documents served contemporaneously with the complaint or answer.

3. Depositions of parties and key witnesses.

4. Depositions of expert witnesses.

5. Physical or mental examinations, if any.

6. Requests to admit.

This scheme is designed primarily to discover facts. It exploits the fact-finding strengths of each of the discovery devices. Interrogatories are served to identify the status, personnel structure and other necessary background information about the adversary, the existence of documents and the identities of lay and expert witnesses. Once this information is disclosed, the discovering party can formulate requests to produce which seek information that actually exists. Further, the disclosure of the adversary's nature and status allows the discovering party to join additional parties. The revelation of key lay and expert witnesses also allows the discovering party to select productive deposition targets.

Under the pyramid approach, depositions are not taken until the deposing party has enough prior information from documents about the deponent to formulate the "right" questions. Finally, the effective deposition of an expert even about a narrow or complex area of the case often requires tremendous background material and preparation. As such, expert depositions are not taken until alternative discovery has been exhausted.

§ 2.15   Developing a Sequence—The Contention Approach

While the pyramid approach to discovery serves the goal of fact-finding or case-building, the "contention" approach to discovery serves the goal of dispute-elimination. The contention approach views discovery as a method of eliminating or reducing the genuine issues of fact between adversaries. Discovery is sequenced in a manner that fosters implicit or explicit admissions. Further, because the ultimate goal of contention discovery is to eliminate the entire dispute among adversaries, the order of discovery should also account for litigation or settlement posturing.

Contention discovery thus may be used as follows:

1. A set of interrogatories served with the initial pleading that includes, (a) contention interrogatories seeking all of the evidence which supports each of the contentions in the adversary's pleadings, and (b) interrogatories seeking the identity of lay and expert witnesses.

2. A notice of deposition for the adversary served with the initial pleading.

3. Requests to admit served with the initial pleading which force the adversary to concede issues at an early stage of the litigation.

4. Notices of deposition immediately served upon each key witness as soon as their identities are known.

This rapid and difficult discovery pace forces the adversary to reveal its case, concede various issues, and makes settlement more attractive. Within this strategic order, the deposition becomes an undesirable alternative to the rapid settlement of the litigation. The strategy is particularly effective when the discovering party moves for summary judgment at a relatively early stage. Under the Supreme Court's summary judgment standard, it is the party *responding* to the summary judgment motion who must obtain "specific facts showing that there is a genuine issue for a trial." *See* Celotex Corp. v. Catrett, 477 U.S. 317, 106 S.Ct. 2548, 91 L.Ed.2d 265 (1986); Fed.R.Civ.P. 56(c). Accordingly, the non-moving party assumes the burden of taking and responding to discovery. Moreover, in responding to the summary judgment motion the nonmoving party must reveal to the moving party most, if not all, of the evidence which supports its theory of the case. Hence, even if the motion is denied, it has the strategic benefit of forcing the non-moving party to disclose its case.

§ 2.16 The Place of Depositions in the Sequence

The decision to depose and the timing of the deposition relative to alternative discovery devices hinges upon the attorney's discovery goals. Where the goal is fact-finding or case-building, the deposition should not be taken until after an adequate informational foundation has been established. Where the goal is dispute reduction, the deposition should be taken of the adversary and its key witnesses as soon as practicable. Form 2–12 provides a discovery sequence chart which can be used in evaluating the proper place of the deposition within the overall discovery plan.

§ 2.17 The Discovery Plan

The definition of discovery goals, the analysis of the effectiveness of each discovery device and the calculation of a proper sequence allow the attorney to develop a successful discovery plan. The ultimate goal of the discovery plan is a resolution of a dispute on terms favorable to the client. The attorney must therefore modify, shorten or enlarge the plan throughout the litigation. Forms 2–13 and 2–14 enable the attorney to keep track of the "fruits" of discovery. They catalogue the information received in light of its value in building the attorney's own case or in destroying the adversary's case. The charts also make lucid the points of authorities which still require some evidentiary support. Accordingly, the charts allow attorneys to take stock in the middle of litigation to determine whether additional discovery, perhaps in the form of depositions, is needed.

Form 2–1

Interrogatory Catalogue

Case _____   Account # _____

Party	Date	Answer Due	Subject Matter	Answer Received	Answer or Objection	Adequacy
			1.			
			2.			
			3.			
			4.			
			5.			
			6.			
			7.			
			8.			
			9.			
			10.			
			11.			
			12.			
			13.			
			14.			
			15.			
			16.			
			17.			
			18.			
			19.			
			20.			
			21.			
			22.			
			23.			

Form 2–2

Interrogatory Responses—Deposition Follow–up

Case _____ Account # _____

Party	Interrogatory	Interrogatory Response	Answer Desired	Deposition Follow-up
	1.			
	2.			
	3.			
	4.			
	5.			
	6.			
	7.			
	8.			
	9.			
	10.			
	11.			
	12.			
	13.			
	14.			
	15.			
	16.			
	17.			
	18.			
	19.			
	20.			
	21.			
	22.			
	23.			

Form 2–3

Requests for Production Catalogue

Case _____   Account # _____

Party _____	Date	Response Due	Subject Matter	Response Received	Response	Adequacy
			1.			
			2.			
			3.			
			4.			
			5.			
			6.			
			7.			
			8.			
			9.			
			10.			
			11.			
			12.			
			13.			
			14.			
			15.			
			16.			
			17.			
			18.			
			19.			
			20.			
			21.			
			22.			
			23.			

Form 2–4

Production Response—Deposition Follow–up

Case _____   Account # _____

Party	Request	Response	Deposition Follow-up	Deposition Exhibit #
	1.			
	2.			
	3.			
	4.			
	5.			
	6.			
	7.			
	8.			
	9.			
	10.			
	11.			
	12.			
	13.			
	14.			
	15.			
	16.			
	17.			
	18.			
	19.			
	20.			
	21.			
	22.			
	23.			

Form 2–5

Physical and Mental Examination Catalogue

Case _____   Account # _____

Party	Exam Requested	Exam Grant	Scope	Report Requested	Report Received	Adversary Report Taken	Adversary Report Requested	Adversary Report Received

Form 2–6

Examination—Deposition Follow-up

Case _____   Account # _____

Party	Exam Results	Adversary Exam Results	Deposition Follow-up	Deposition Response

Form 2–7

Requests to Admit Catalogue

Case _____   Account # _____

Party	Request Served	Response Due	Request	Response	Adequacy
			1.		
			2.		
			3.		
			4.		
			5.		
			6.		
			7.		
			8.		
			9.		
			10.		
			11.		
			12.		
			13.		
			14.		
			15.		
			16.		
			17.		
			18.		
			19.		
			20.		
			21.		
			22.		
			23.		

Form 2–8

Requests to Admit—Deposition Follow–up

Case _____   Account # _____

Party	Request	Request Response	Deposition Follow-up
	1.		
	2.		
	3.		
	4.		
	5.		
	6.		
	7.		
	8.		
	9.		
	10.		
	11.		
	12.		
	13.		
	14.		
	15.		
	16.		
	17.		
	18.		
	19.		
	20.		
	21.		
	22.		
	23.		

Form 2–9

Written Deposition Catalogue

Case _____   Account # _____

Witness	Notice Served & Subpoena Served	Response	Deposition Date/Time	Transcript Received	Deposition Signed	Deposition Filed

Form 2–10

Oral Deposition Catalogue

Case _____   Account # _____

Witness	Notice Served & Subpoena Served	Response	Deposition Date/Time	Transcript Received	Deposition Signed	Deposition Filed

Discovery Alternatives Chart

Method	Definition	Party or Nonparty	Timing	Response	Method of Service
Interrogatories	Series of written questions served by a party which must be answered fully and separately, in writing and under oath. Fed.R.Civ. P. 33(a).	Party only; but may use written depositions for non-parties. Fed.R.Civ. P. 33(a); 31.	Anytime, including with the complaint. Fed.R.Civ. P. 33(a).	30 Days; 45 days if served with complaint. Fed.R.Civ. P. 33(a).	Mail
Requests for Production	A party may serve upon another party a request to produce, or to enter land to inspect, documents or tangible thing in the possession, custody or control of the other party. Fed.R.Civ. P. 34(a).	Party only; but may accompany notice of deposition of a non-party with a Rule 45 subpoena for documents. Fed.R.Civ. P. 45.	Anytime; including with the complaint. Fed.R.Civ. P. 34.	30 days; 45 days if served with the complaint. Fed.R.Civ. P. 34.	Mail
Physical and Mental Examinations	A party may move to compel another party to undergo a mental or physical examination. Fed.R. Civ. P. 35(a).	Party or its agents only. Fed.R.Civ. P. 35(a).	Anytime, with leave. Fed.R.Civ. P. 35(a).	Specified in court order. Fed.R.Civ. P. 35(a).	Court order; detailed written report of findings must be delivered. Fed.R.Civ. P. 35(b).
Requests to Admit	A party may serve on another party a request that the other party admit opinions, facts, the application of law to fact or the genuineness of documents. Fed. R.Civ. P. 36.	Party only. Fed.R. Civ. P. 36.	Anytime, including with complaint. Fed. R.Civ. P. 36(a).	30 days; 45 days if served with complaint. Admitted if not denied. Fed.R. Civ. P. 36(a).	Mail
Written Deposition	A party may take and record the testimony of any person by compelling the person to answer a series of written questions under oath. Fed.R.Civ. P. 31.	Written deposition may be taken of both parties and non-parties. Fed.R. Civ. P. 31(a).	Before commencement of the action with leave of court to perpetuate testimony Fed.R.Civ. P. 27. After commencement of the action, they may be taken at any time. Fed.R.Civ. P. 31.	At a reasonable and convenient time, typically by agreement.	
Oral Deposition	A party may take and record the testimony of any person upon oral examination. Fed.R.Civ. P. 30.	Oral deposition may be taken of both parties and non-parties. Fed.R.Civ. P. 30(a).	Before commencement of the action, with leave of court to perpetuate testimony. Fed.R.Civ. P. 27. After commencement of the action, at any time. Fed.R.Civ. P. 31.	At a reasonable and convenient time, typically by agreement.	

Method	Leave of Court Required	Control of Response or Follow-up	Expense	Efficacy	Use at Trial	Notes
Interrogatories	no	none	minimal	—general background information, —identity of lay and expert witnesses; —status of other parties —contention interrogatories	—Evidentiary Admissions; impeachment.	
Requests for Production	no	none	moderate particularly in organization and review of documents.	—discovery of candid information from an adversary prepared before litigation. —discovery of business records which can be admitted at trial.	—Exhibits admissible under business record exception to the hearsay cite rule.	
Physical and Mental Examinations	yes; affirmative showing of good cause to take exam and that the material discovered is probative of an issue in controversy.	none	significant; examining physician is an expert who must be reimbursed.	—produce unalterable evidence of physical or mental condition; —have great settlement value —may induce the elimination of issues in controversy.	—Admissibility at trial as an expert's report.	
Requests to Admit	no	none; but self-executing sanction for failure to respond.	minimal	—eliminate matters not in dispute —obtain admissions for use at trial —obtain admissions for use in summary judgment.	—Conclusive admissions at trial.	
Written Deposition	no, unless sought before commencement of action to perpetuate testimony, Fed.R.Civ. P. 27, 31, or sought as to an expert witness. Fed.R.Civ. P. 26.	little; may serve follow-up questions. Fed.R.Civ. P. 31(a).	minimal	—functional equivalent of interrogatories for non-parties —functional equivalent of document request for non-parties when accompanied by Rule 45 subpoena —cost effective alternative to oral depositions —record of testimony of unavailable, minor or friendly witness.	—Deposition of a party or unavailable non-party by adverse party for any purpose —Deposition of an available non-party used mainly for impeachment.	
Oral Deposition	no, unless sought before commencement of action to perpetuate testimony, Fed.R.Civ. P. 27, 30, or sought as to an expert witness. Fed.R.Civ. P. 26.	substantial	significant	—parties and key witnesses —discovery of detailed litigation-provoking facts —party, rather than attorney, responds —establish and lock-in adverse version of facts —assess demeanor of witness —insight into trial.	—Deposition of a party of unavailable non-party used by an adverse party for any purpose. —Deposition of an available non-party used mainly for impeachment.	

Form 2–11 (continued)

Discovery Sequence Chart

Method	Limit on Discovery Sequencing	Role in Fact-Building	Role in Dispute-Reduction	Notes
Interrogatories	1. If served with complaint, defendant has 45 days to respond. Fed.R.Civ. P. 33. 2. Court may shorten or enlarge time for responding. Fed.R.Civ. P. 33. 3. Court may order that contention interrogatories not be answered until "after designated discovery." Fed. R.Civ. P. 33(b). 4. Rule 26(c) protective order 5. Rule 26(d) sequencing	1. Identities of lay and expert witnesses 2. Existence of documents 3. Reveal status and employment structure of adversary 4. Disclose related events or transaction	1. Contention interrogatories 2. Identities of lay and expert witnesses	
Requests to Produce	1. If served with complaint, defendant has 45 days to respond. Fed.R.Civ. P. 34. 2. Court may shorten or enlarge time for responding. Fed.R.Civ. P. 34. 3. Rule 26(c) protective order 4. Rule 26(d) sequencing	1. Pre-litigation records of parties 2. Background memoranda	1. Admissions in business records 2. Smoking guns 3. Disclosure of privileged information 4. Creates burdens, particularly for small businesses	
Physical and Mental Examinations	1. Alternative methods of discovery explored first. Fed.R.Civ. P. 35. 2. Rule 26(c) protective order 3. Rule 26(d) sequencing	1. Evidence of mental or physical condition of parties, where condition is in controversy	1. Induces admissions of matters previously in controversy 2. Induces settlement	

Method	Limit on Discovery Sequencing	Role in Fact-Building	Role in Dispute-Reduction	Notes
Requests to Admit	1. If served with complaint, defendant has 45 days to respond. Fed. R.Civ. P. 36. 2. Court may shorten or enlarge time for response. Fed.R.Civ. P. 36 3. Although Rule 36 limits the availability of the "lack of information" response to a request to admit, that response if more plausible at an early stage of litigation. 4. Rule 26(c) protective order 5. Rule 26(d) sequencing	1. Genuineness of documents 2. Fact Admissions	1. Eliminates issues in dispute 2. Sets up summary judgment	
Written Depositions	1. Notice; custom of reasonableness and convenience 2. Rule 26(c) protective order 3. Rule 26(d) sequencing	1. To perpetuate testimony if before action. 2. Interrogatories for non-parties 3. Document request for non-parties 4. Record of testimony for unavailable, minor or unfriendly witnesses.	1. Admissions 2. Locking testimony 3. Impeachment	
Oral Depositions	1. Notice; custom of reasonableness and convenience	1. Discovery of detailed litigation provoking facts 2. Discovery of information from parties and key witnesses	1. Testimony from party rather than attorney. 2. Establish and lock-in adversary's version of facts 3. Assess witness demeanor 4. Intimidation 5. Insight into trial behavior 6. Impeachment 7. Admissions 8. Use at trial against adversary for any purpose	

Form 2–12 (continued)

Form 2–13

The Fruits of Discovery—Claims

Case _____   Account # _____

Specific Claim: _____

Elements of Claim	Supporting Law	Supporting Discovery	Needed Discovery
1.			
2.			
3.			
4.			
5.			

The Fruits of Discovery—Defenses

Case _____   Account # _____

Specific Defense: _____

Elements of Defense	Supporting Law	Supporting Discovery	Needed Discovery
1.			
2.			
3.			
4.			
5.			

Chapter 3

MATTERS TO CONSIDER BEFORE THE DEPOSITION

Table of Sections

---

§ 3.1 Generally

After the attorney has decided to depose a witness, he must ensure that various procedural requirements have been met. The deposing attorney must first establish a proper time and location for the deposition. The attorney then must serve notice and subpoenas. When the time and place of the deposition have been established, the attorney should determine the best method of, and arrange for, presentation of the record. Finally, the deposing attorney should consider who should accompany him to the deposition.

§ 3.2 Timing

A deposition may be taken of any lay witness without leave of court at any time after the commencement of the action. Fed.R.Civ.P. 30(a). A court order is required, however, if the plaintiff wants to take a deposition less than thirty days after filing the complaint. Fed.R.Civ. P. 30(a). No court order is necessary if the defendant has already noticed the plaintiff's deposition, or if the notice states that the deponent is "about" to become unavailable. Fed.R. Civ.P. 30(b)(2). Under the "special notice" provisions of Federal Rule 30(b)(2), the plaintiff may take a deposition within the initial 30–day period without leave of court if the notice includes a "statement" that the deponent will be unavailable after that period because he is (1) about to go out of the district where the action is pending and more than 100 miles from the place of trial, (2) about to go out of the United States, or (3) about to go on a voyage at sea. The notice must also include facts supporting the claimed unavailability of the deponent. The attorney's signature on the notice is a warrant that to the best of his knowledge, information and belief, the statement and the supporting facts are true. A notice signed in violation of this rule is tantamount to a violation of Fed.R.Civ.P. 11.

A deposition may not be taken without leave of court, as well, when it is taken to perpetuate testimony before the commencement of the action. Fed.R.Civ.P. 27(a). By its very nature, such a deposition cannot be taken at an optimal time. While the petition requesting leave to take a deposition before the action need not state that the deponent is about to become unavailable, the petition must satisfy the judge that the "purpose" for the deposition is compelling. Fed.R.Civ.P. 27(a). That "purpose" is often the imminent unavailability of the deponent. Hence, time is typically of the essence in requesting such a deposition.

Moreover, the process of obtaining the pre-commencement deposition is time-consuming. First, the petition must be filed in the district court in which the deponent resides. Second, notice of the deposition must be served on each person named in the petition as an expected adverse party, not just the deponent. Third, notice must be served at least 20 days before the deposition date. Fourth, the process contemplates a "hearing" to determine whether such a deposition may be taken. Fed.R.Civ.P. 27(a). In light of this lengthy procedure and the typically imminent unavailability of the prospective deponent, attorneys seeking to depose witnesses before commencing an action must exercise considerable forethought.

Finally, the attorney's discretion to depose witnesses at any time is also limited when the deponent is an expert witness. Although Fed.R.Civ.P. 26(b)(4) freely allows interrogatories to determine identities and subjects of expert witnesses, it permits depositions of such experts only upon "motion." The Rules contemplate a two-step discovery process. Expert depositions take place only after initial interrogatories have been served and answered. Attorneys, therefore, cannot even consider moving for the deposition of an expert witness until 45 days after the complaint has been served. Forms 3–1 thru 3–4 present the timing requirements for each type of deposition. Form 3–5 catalogues the alternative deposition locations.

§ 3.3 Notice—Generally

Every deposition must be properly noticed. The requirements for proper notice, however, vary depending on whether the deposition is (1) before the action, (2) within 30 days of filing the complaint, (3) upon written questions, or (4) oral.

The lawyer schedules a deposition by serving a notice which states an intention to depose a certain witness. Fed.R.Civ.P. 30(b)(1). Notice must include the name and address of the deponent, if known, and the date, time and place of deposition. Parties may vary the form of notice by *written* stipulation. Fed.R.Civ.P. 29(1). If the deponent is a party, the service of notice sufficient to require his/her appearance at deposition and a subpoena is unnecessary. Fed.R.Civ.P. 37(d). Notice may be accompanied by a request that documents and tangible items be produced at deposition, in which event, the procedure of Rule 34 applies. Fed.R.Civ. P. 30(b)(5). It is not clear whether the 30–day response period of Rule 34 applies to a request for production under 30(b)(5). *See* Wright & Miller, Federal Practice and Procedure § 2108. If the deponent is not a party, he should be served with a subpoena. Fed.R.Civ.P. 30(a), 45. If a witness fails to appear because no subpoena is issued, a court may impose costs of other counsel upon the party giving notice of the deposition. If a subpoena duces tecum is to be served on a deponent, the notice should include, or have attached to it, a designation of the materials to be produced. Fed.R.Civ.P. 30(b)(1). The rationale of this requirement is to enable each party to prepare for the deposition more effectively. Other counsel may request that the deposition be taken at a location other than that designated in the notice. Fed.R.Civ.P. 26(c)(2). Or, other counsel may accept designation of place but argue that the serving party should pay witness's or counsel's travel expenses in connection with the deposition. A party serving notice for deposition of a witness, party or nonparty, *outside* the jurisdiction where the case is pending should recognize the substantial danger that he will receive a request from some other party for reimbursement of its travel and related expenses.

A party seeking to depose an opponent's expert must usually pay him a reasonable fee for the time he spends responding to discovery. Fed.R.Civ.P. 26(b)(4)(c)(i). Such payment may be required not only for the time during which the expert is being deposed, but also for preparation and travel time. Fed.R.Civ.P. 26(b)(c)(ii). The privilege of deposing a party's expert may be made contingent by the court upon compensation to that party of a "fair portion" of the expert's fee. This compensation is in addition to that paid to the expert for his time and may be ordered by the court either before or after the discovery from the expert is completed.

The notice may name as deponent a corporation, partnership, association or governmental agency and should describe with reasonable particularity the matters on which examination is sought. Fed.R.Civ.P. 30(b)(6). The organization named must then designate one or more officers, directors, managing agents, or other persons who consent to testify for the organization to appear at the deposition.

Federal Rule of Civil Procedure 37(a)(2) provides for an order compelling designation. It may be easier to use this procedure to compel the organization to identify a witness than to select a name based on limited information with hope that the witness will be sufficiently knowledgeable. The rule dispenses with the need to depose many witnesses in the search for those with relevant knowledge. Of course, if the organization is an adverse party, it may not identify the most knowledgeable or helpful witness to appear at deposition.

§ 3.4 Notice of Deposition Before Action

In order to take a deposition to perpetuate testimony before an action, an attorney must file a petition and serve notice. Fed.R.Civ.P. 27(a). The petition must be verified and filed in the district court of any party expected to be adverse. The petition is captioned in the name of the person desiring the deposition. The attorney must seek an order authorizing the deposition to perpetuate testimony and include:

1. a statement that the petitioner expects to be a party in an action;
2. a statement that the action is one over which the federal courts have subject matter jurisdiction;
3. a statement that the petitioner is currently unable to bring the action;
4. the facts which the deposition is designed to establish;
5. the reasons for desiring to perpetuate the testimony;
6. the names or descriptions of persons whom the petitioner expects to be adverse parties;
7. the addresses of the expected adverse parties, if known;
8. the names and addresses of the prospective deponents; and
9. the substance of the testimony expected from each deponent.

A copy of this petition, together with notice, must be served upon each expected adverse party. The "notice" should reiterate the names and addresses, if known, of the prospective deponents and must state the time and place for the deposition. Fed.R.Civ.P. 30(b). Unlike routine deposition notice, however, the notice of a deposition to perpetuate testimony must be served with the petition at least 20 days before the hearing to determine whether the depositions should be taken.

The notice and petition must be served upon each expected adverse party named in the petition in accordance with Fed.R.Civ.P. 4(d). Thus, service may be made:

1. personally on the expected adverse party, other than an infant or incompetent person;

2. leaving the notice and petition at the expected adverse party's usual place of abode with someone of suitable age and discretion;

3. delivering the notice and petition to an agent authorized to receive service;

4. delivering a copy of the notice and petition upon an officer or agent authorized to receive process of an expected adverse corporation, partnership or association;

5. by mailing two copies of the notice and petition to the expected adverse parties together with an acknowledgment and a return, postage pre-paid envelope addressed to the sender; or

6. in accordance with the law of the state in which the district court sits.

If, however, service of the petition and notice by one of these methods cannot be made with due diligence, the district court may order alternative service, including by way of publication. Fed.R.Civ.P. 27(a). When service under Fed.R.Civ.P. 4(d) cannot be made and alternative service is required, the court must appoint an attorney to represent each non-served, adverse party. Moreover, the court itself must cross-examine the deponent if expected adverse parties are not otherwise represented. Fed.R.Civ.P. 27(a).

§ 3.5 Special Notice for Deposition Within 30 Days of Service of Complaint

A plaintiff wishing to take a deposition within 30 days of service of the complaint, without leave of court, and where the defendant has not yet sought discovery, must serve "special notice" to each party. The special notice, in addition to providing the usual place, time, names and addresses, must state that the deponent (1) is about to go out of the district where the action is pending and more than 100 miles from the place of trial, (2) is about to go out of the country, or (3) is at sea. Fed.R.Civ.P. 30(b)(2). The notice must include facts supporting the claimed unavailability of the deponent. Moreover, the special notice must be signed by the attorney which warrants that the contents of the notice are true. *Id.* Fed.R.Civ.P. 11 sanctions may be entered against an attorney who signs the special notice without a reasonable belief that the statements in the notice are accurate.

This special notice must be served upon the deponent and upon every party to the action within a reasonable time before the deposition itself. Notice is served pursuant to Fed.R.Civ.P. 5 by delivering it to the party or its attorney, through (a) hand-delivery, (b) leaving it with a clerk or other person in charge at the office of the party or attorney, (c) if no one is in charge, leaving it at that office in a "conspicuous" place, or (d) if the office is closed, leaving it at the party's home or usual abode with someone of suitable age and discretion. Alternatively, the special notice may be mailed to the attorney or party at either's last known address. Finally, if the addresses of the attorney and party are unknown, notice may be served by leaving it with the clerk of court. The notice of deposition must be filed with the court either before service or within a reasonable time after service. Fed.R.Civ.P. 5(d). Local rules and practices, however, have modified this rule, generally providing that discovery not be filed with the court.

§ 3.6 Notice of Written Deposition

Notice of a written deposition taken more than 30 days after the filing of the complaint must also be served in accordance with Fed.R.Civ.P. 5 on the deponent and every party to the action. Fed.R.Civ.P. 31(a). In addition, however, the discovering party must actually serve upon the deponent and the parties copies of the written deposition questions. *Id.* Furthermore, the notice must include:

1. the deponent's name;
2. the deponent's address;
3. a general description of the deponent or of the group to which he belongs if his name is unknown;
4. the name or title of the officer before whom the deposition is to be taken.

The notice may, but is not required to, include the date, time and place of the deposition. The officer may take on the responsibility of setting up the deposition. Accordingly, the deposing party must deliver a copy of the notice and of the written questions to the designated officer. The officer then must "proceed promptly" to take the deposition.

§ 3.7 Notice of Oral Deposition—Generally

The typical deposition is taken orally, and more than 30 days after service of the complaint. For these depositions, "reasonable notice" must be given to the deponent and every party to the action. Fed.R.Civ.P. 30(b)(1).

Reasonable notice has two components: information and time. Fed.R.Civ.P. 30(b)(1) requires that notice include the following information:

(1) place of deposition;

(2) time of deposition;

(3) deponent's name;

(4) deponent's address;

(5) a general description of deponent sufficient to identify him, if his name is not known; and

(6) the materials to be produced at the deposition if a subpoena duces tecum has been served.

The notice, however, may be imprecise regarding all of this required information. For example, the deposition can be noticed at a "mutually convenient place to be agreed to later" and can be scheduled to continue generally from day to day until completion. *See,* 8 Wright & Miller, Federal Practice and Procedure, § 2111. The deponent's name and address may be omitted if not known. Moreover, an organization may be asked to designate a deponent who is most knowledgeable to testify to certain matters. Fed.R.Civ.P. 30(b)(3). Thus, despite the formal requirements of information in the notice, the courts have allowed the parties considerable latitude to conduct discovery in a mutually beneficial and professional manner. *Id.*

The Federal Rules do not contain formal requirements for the timing of notice. What constitutes a "reasonable" time will be assessed on a case-by-case basis. In the typical case with a relatively lengthy discovery period, reasonable notice is no less than five days before the examination. *See* Wright & Miller, at § 2111. But where the court has ordered expedited discovery such as in hotly contested corporate takeover litigation, "reasonable" notice becomes a period of hours.

Whether notice is vague or precise, relaxed or expedited, the standard of reasonableness will be informed by the over-arching goals of the Federal Rules. These Rules are designed to foster the just and efficient resolution of disputes based upon their merits, rather than upon hypertechnical rules of pleading. *See* Fed.R.Civ.P. 1. Meritorious dispute resolution requires the clash of two prepared adversaries. Thus, deposition notice is reasonable under the Federal Rules if it affords the deponent an opportunity to prepare for the deposition and the deponent's attorney an opportunity to prepare to question the witness.

§ 3.8 Notice to Party Deponents

Reasonable notice given to a party pursuant to Fed.R.Civ.P. 5 is generally sufficient to compel the party's attendance at the deposition. The failure of the party to attend his deposition will result in the sanctions of Fed.R.Civ.P. 37(d). Those sanctions include: an order that facts adverse to the non-appearing deponent be admitted, prohibiting the non-appearing deponent from introducing certain evidence, striking claims or defenses, staying proceedings, or dismissing the action. The court also has discretion to sanction non-attendance by entering any other order it deems just or awarding appropriate attorneys fees.

Moreover, under Fed.R. of Civ.P. 30(b)(5) notice to a party which includes a request made in compliance with Fed.R.Civ.P. 34 for the production of documents is sufficient to compel that production. The Advisory Committee Notes to Fed.R.Civ.P. 30(b)(5) caution that where the documents requested are "many and complex," the deponent may seek a court order that productions be accomplished under the traditional Fed.R.Civ.P. 34 procedures. The notice of deposition to a party individual can and should include a request to bring to deposition those documents which are "closely related to the oral examination." Adv.Comm. Notes, Fed.R.Civ. P. 30(b)(5). Forms 3–6 and 3–7 are examples of sufficient notice to an individual and organizational party.

When the deposition of an individual or organization party is to be taken by other than stenographic means, such as by videotape, the notice should contain evidence of a stipulation or court order permitting such alternative means. The stipulation or order which is included in the notice must designate the person before whom the deposition is to be taken, the method of preserving the testimony and the manner of filing the deposition. Fed.R.Civ.P. 30(b)(4). It may also contain an indication of additional procedures which will be used to ensure the accuracy of the recorded testimony. Form 3–8 provides sufficient notice for the taking of an oral deposition by other than stenographic means.

§ 3.9 Notice to Non-party Deponents

When the deponent is not a party, the sanctions of Fed.R.Civ.P. 37(d) are inadequate to compel deposition attendance. A subpoena must issue to compel the attendance of a non-party witness. The fact that a subpoena is issued, however, does not relieve the deposing party of the duty to provide reasonable notice to every other party to the action. *See* Fed.R.Civ.P. 30(b)(1). Hence, when a non-party is to be deposed, the deposing party must both serve a subpoena on the deponent and provide notice.

To depose a *non-party* witness under a subpoena in a location outside the forum, have the notice certified and sent to the court of general jurisdiction where the witness resides. In the federal system (and in many state courts), proof of service of the notice of deposition must be submitted to the court with jurisdiction over the case. That court certifies the notice and then transmits it, together with a subpoena, to the clerk of the court having jurisdiction over the deponent for issuance and service by the marshal.

The recipient of a notice of deposition can rarely avoid the deposition. Courts have rejected arguments that a deposition would be unnecessarily costly or time-consuming, that a deposition was already taken, or that some other form of discovery would suffice. Quashing the deposition notice requires its being shown to be both totally irrelevant and being taken as a means of harassment.

Usually, a more promising response will be a motion for a protective order under Fed.R. Civ.P. 26(c). The attorney may ask the court to limit the scope of deposition, to protect the privacy of deposition, to seal the transcript to preserve confidentiality, to postpone discovery pending resolution of preliminary questions, or to decide in advance questions of cost, timing and location. Since the motion effectively stays the taking of a deposition, prudence and good faith suggest that motions for protection be filed early. Do not wait until the eve of the deposition.

Unlike Fed.R.Civ.P. 30 which covers party depositions, Fed.R.Civ.P. 45 requires a subpoena to compel a non-party's attendance at a deposition. Deposition Subpoenas are provided in

Forms 3–9 and 3–10. There are two types of Fed.R.Civ.P. 45 deposition subpoenas: the subpoena *ad testificandum* which requires merely that the deponent attend and give testimony and the subpoena *duces tecum* which also requires the witness to bring specified documents or other items. The first step in taking a Fed.R.Civ.P. 45 deposition is serving a notice of the deposition on all parties, in any manner authorized by Fed.R.Civ.P. 30. Next, a subpoena form and any necessary attachments, such as a schedule of documents, is prepared and taken to the clerk, along with a copy of the notice of deposition and a certificate of service. After receiving proof of service of notice and usually taking a copy of notice for filing, the clerk will issue the subpoena by affixing his official seal or stamp.

It is only slightly more complicated if the deposition is to be taken outside the district where the case is pending. First, serve the notice of deposition in the district of the pending case. Then, if local rules permit or require the filing of discovery documents, file a copy of the notice and accompanying certificate of service with the clerk in the same district.

§ 3.10 Notice Outside the District

Demonstrate to the clerk in the *outside* district that notice has been served in the first district by showing him a copy of the notice and either a duplicate original or a certified copy of the certificate of service. Find out in advance by telephone or local counsel what the clerk requires for the issuance of a subpoena. Some clerks demand an original certificate of service; to others, a copy is enough. Once the clerk has the required papers, he issues a subpoena for service on the witness in the outside district. Requests for production under Fed.R.Civ.P. 34 do not work with non-parties, so it is necessary to use a subpoena duces tecum. This kind of subpoena must describe the documents or other things that the witness is supposed to bring to the deposition. There is space on the subpoena form for this description, but because the space is small, the usual practice is to attach a schedule listing the requested items.

Once the subpoena has been issued it must be served on the prospective witness. In addition to the subpoena and its attachments, the notice of deposition may be served, although it is not mandatory.

Subpoenas may be served by anyone 18 years of age or older and not a party, and must be personally served on the witness. Fed.R.Civ.P. 45(c).

An attorney who seeks to depose a party to a lawsuit must provide reasonable written notice to all parties in the action. *See* Fed.R.Civ.P. 30(b). The notice must specify the time and place of the deposition and the name of the person to be deposed. The original scheduled deposition date or time is often continued or modified from the original notice date. Thus, the attorneys maintain an appearance of diligence, although there is no intent to proceed with the deposition until a later date. Agreements regarding notice may be made between the attorneys, though they must be in accordance with Fed.R.Civ.P. 29 and are usually handled over the telephone and through written confirmation.

The attendance of a non-party deponent can be compelled only through the issuance of a subpoena (*see* Fed.R.Civ.P. 45(a)). As a rule, non-party witnesses are not required to travel long distances for deposition merely for the convenience of the attorneys or parties. Corporate executives will usually be deposed at their place of business with other non-party witnesses being deposed in their own area of residence. While an attorney is not *required* to attend the deposition of a non-party witness (nor even of a non-client party, so long as s/he did not notice the deposition), the attorney risks waiving any objections or questioning opportunity of that witness. The attorney may arrange for another attorney to be present at the deposition to act as a proxy and ask specified questions for the absent counsel; good relations between the attorneys is a pre-requisite to any such arrangement.

§ 3.11 Notice of Foreign Oral Deposition

For depositions taken outside the judicial system in which the action is pending (either out-of-state in a state court action or out of the United States in a federal action), the methods of noticing a deposition and compelling attendance are more complex.

§ 3.12 Out–of–State Deposition

The forum state must engage in some act empowering the issuance of a subpoena in the state in which the deposition is to be taken. Each state has developed its own procedures for the taking of out-of-state depositions. *See* Appendix A. Typically, the forum state will issue a commission to the officer before whom the deposition will be taken. The commission empowers the court reporter to issue a subpoena, to record the testimony and to file the deposition. Form 3–11 is an example of a motion to obtain such a commission.

§ 3.13 Depositions Outside the United States

Depositions may be taken in a foreign country if the deposing party:

(1) obtains a commission;

(2) obtains a "letter rogatory";

(3) serves notice and takes the deposition before a person authorized to administer oaths; *or*

(4) obtains a stipulation.

The commission is an order issued by a court of the United States which authorizes a designated individual to take the deposition of a named witness. Often in multi-national actions, a district court will appoint a magistrate for the purpose of overseeing depositions in a foreign country.

Alternatively, the Federal Rules permit the taking of foreign depositions by letters rogatory. A letter rogatory is a request issued by a United States court to a foreign authority that the foreign authority allow the taking of a deposition within the foreign territory. Finally, and most simply, a foreign deposition may be taken upon reasonable notice or by stipulation—just as a domestic deposition.

That the Federal Rules authorize foreign depositions upon any one of these procedures, however, is only half of the battle. The foreign state must also cooperate in the deposition process. Simple notice, for example, will rarely comport with the law of the foreign jurisdiction. For its many signatories, the Hague Convention for the Taking of Evidence Abroad in Civil or Commercial Matters, Vol. 8, Part VII, Martindale–Hubble Law Directory (1988), governs the acceptable method of taking a foreign deposition. That Convention permits the taking of a deposition either by way of "Letters of Request," or by way of diplomatic officers, consular agents or other commissioners. A Letter of Request can be used to obtain *evidence*, rather than simply the names of potential witnesses for example, which is actually intended to be used in pending or contemplated judicial actions. It should be in the language of the foreign state and *must* state:

(1) the requesting and the requested authority;

(2) the names and addresses of parties, if known;

(3) the nature of the proceedings;

(4) the evidence to be obtained;

(5) the names and addresses of the persons to be examined;

(6) the questions to be put to the persons examined and the nature of the subject matter of the examination;

(7) documents to be inspected; and

(8) the nature of the oath to be administered.

Although the Convention does not set forth requirements for the taking of evidence by a diplomatic officer, consular agent or other commissioner, the application for such a commission should track the requirements for a Letter of Request. The taking of evidence without a Letter of Request is, under the terms of the Convention, limited to proceedings already "commenced."

Fed.R.Civ.P. 28(b) anticipates some of the problems associated with the taking of foreign depositions. It allows the use of those depositions in United States Courts even if they are not verbatim accounts of the testimony or whether they bear the peculiar mark of the foreign customs. Nonetheless, the process of securing a foreign deposition is a difficult and potentially expensive one. Attorneys are best advised to contact local counsel in the foreign state and the State Department before attempting to take a foreign deposition. Moreover, attorneys should make sure prior to incurring the expense of such a deposition that they have explored all alternative methods of obtaining the same evidence. Forms 3–12 and 3–13 provide common, alternative methods for obtaining foreign depositions.

§ 3.14 Deposition Subpoena: Issue and Service

A subpoena to compel attendance at a deposition or a subpoena duces tecum for the production of documents must be issued by the clerk of the district court for the district in which the deposition is to be taken. Fed.R.Civ.P. 45(d). The local rules in each district govern the proper issuance by the clerk of subpoenas. The subpoena cannot issue unless proof of service of notice to take the deposition is given to the clerk. Such proof is established by filing the notice of deposition in the proper court, together with a statement of the (1) date of service, (2) means of service, (3) names of persons served, and (4) certificate of service, Fed.R.Civ.P. 45(d)(1). When a subpoena deces tecum is sought, both the notice and the subpoena must contain a reasonably specific list of the documents requested to be produced at deposition.

Once the subpoena is issued, it must be properly served. Local rules govern the methods of service. But it must be served by a non-party older than 18 years of age by delivery to the deponent. Fed.R.Civ.P. 45(c). Typically, a private process server will be authorized to effect service. The subpoena may require any person to attend deposition at any place within 100 miles of where he (1) works, (2) transacts business, or (3) is served. In addition, the court may order the deposition of a non-party to be conducted at any other convenient place, Fed.R.Civ.P. 45(d).

Issue of a subpoena for a non-party witness should not be done lightly. For example, service of a subpoena may offend an otherwise friendly witness. In an effort to keep relations amicable, some attorneys arrange for a non-party deposition by "loose agreement;" such an agreement is dangerous. First, friendly witnesses often become unfriendly as the litigation progresses. Second, absent a subpoena, there is no way to compel the attendance of the non-party witness or to sanction his improper termination of the deposition. Third, the subpoena requires the non-party witness to bring to the deposition documents which he cannot otherwise be compelled to produce. Finally, the issuance of a subpoena has the salutary effect of reinforcing even in the most friendly witness the formality of the deposition process. If the attorney wishes to reduce the sting created by the service of a subpoena, he may want to provide the witness with a courtesy note or call in advance of the service. But the attorney should not sidestep the requirements of the Federal Rules. Forms 3–9 and 3–10 may be used to compel the attendance of a non-party witness at deposition.

§ 3.15 Serving the Notice of Deposition

Attorneys should make arrangements with the witness and other lawyers before actually serving a notice of deposition. Many of the problems that occur during depositions can be prevented by serving timely notice. For example, notice for the week of annual vacation is a surefire way to antagonize the witness or the opposing lawyer.

The Federal Rules require only reasonable notice. The notice provided in Form 3–6 is an example. Local rules and decisions usually determine what is reasonable notice. Most common periods are five to seven days for local depositions and ten days for depositions in other jurisdictions. When notice of deposition to a non-party witness is accompanied by a subpoena duces tecum, Fed.R.Civ.P. 45(d)(1) ordinarily grants the witness ten days to object to the inspection or copying of documents sought by the subpoena.

In cases where the notice of deposition is unenforceable unless accompanied by subpoena, attorneys should have the subpoena served even if the witness is cooperative. Then if the deponent fails to show up, penalties described in Fed.R.Civ.P. 30(g)(2) can be avoided. To soften the sting of a subpoena, explain that it was served for the witness's protection, to ensure payment of statutory fees, and to give him clear justification to be absent from work.

§ 3.16 Location—Generally

Attorneys should select the best location for the deposition that the rules will allow. Accordingly, the attorney must first determine which geographical locations are proper. Then, the attorney should decide which of the proper geographic locations is the best strategic location. Finally, attorneys must select an optimal site within that geographic location. Form 3–14 provides a vehicle for analyzing each of these concerns.

§ 3.17 Proper Location

The Federal Rules governing depositions do not require that they be held in any specific location. Fed.R.Civ.P. 45(d) governs subpoenas for taking depositions and does limit the reach of those subpoenas. A person upon whom a deposition subpoena has been served cannot be required to attend the deposition at any place greater than 100 miles from the place of his employment, the place where he transacts business or the place where he was served. Alternatively, Fed.R.Civ.P. 45(d) allows the court, by order, to fix another "convenient" location for the deposition.

The question of proper deposition location, therefore, hinges on whether a Fed.R.Civ.P. 45(d) subpoena must be served. The Federal Rules do not require that a subpoena be served, even as to non-party deponents. Hence, it is possible to take the deposition of parties and non-parties in any geographic location. It is not possible, however, to *compel* the attendance of a non-party witness at a deposition without a subpoena. Fed.R.Civ.P. 37(d) provides its own sanctions for a *party's* failure to attend at his own deposition. The sanctions, the most severe of which is default, however, are discretionary and difficult to obtain. This Rule also provides sanctions for the failure of a party's agent, director, managing agent or testifying agent to appear at deposition. This Rule does not, however, provide any sanction for the failure of a person other than a party, or its officer, director, managing agent or testifying agent to appear at a deposition. Accordingly, the attendance of such a person can only be compelled by a Fed.R.Civ.P. 45(d) subpoena. The sanction for failing to comply with a subpoena is contempt (Fed.R.Civ.P. 45(f)) and can be avoided only if there is an "adequate excuse" such as an *inability* to comply.

Together, the Federal Rules suggest the following location guidelines:

1. The deposition of a party can be held in any geographic location because the non-attendance of the party can be sanctioned under Fed.R.Civ.P. 37(d).

2. Because a person not a party or officer, director, managing agent or testifying agent of a party cannot be compelled to appear at a deposition without a subpoena and because the subpoena requires the deposition to be taken within 100 miles of that person's residence, business, service or employment, attorneys should serve such a subpoena and fix the deposition location within those boundaries.

Although a Fed.R.Civ.P. 45(d) subpoena is not needed to compel a party's attendance at a deposition, attorneys should nevertheless consider having one issue. The subpoena's contempt sanction adds teeth to Fed.R.Civ.P. 37(d) sanctions.

Whether attendance has been compelled pursuant to notice or subpoena, the Rules allow the prospective deponent to attempt a change in the deposition's location. Fed.R.Civ.P. 26(c)(2) empowers the court to enter a protective order, setting the place of discovery. Further, the court may modify the place of deposition in response to a motion to quash the subpoena. The court has wide discretion to fix the place of deposition, so long as the motion for a protective order or to quash the subpoena is made seasonably.

In exercising its discretion, the district court will be guided by these presumptions: the plaintiff should be available for deposition in the district where the suit was filed and a defendant corporation should be deposed at its principal place of business. *See* Wright &

Miller, 8 Federal Practice and Procedure, § 2112. Apart from these presumptions, courts weigh the financial hardship to both parties in deciding to alter location, and have on occasion required the payment of travel expenses. *Id.; see also* Thompson v. Sun Oil Co., 523 F.2d 647 (8th Cir.1975).

Although the Rules favor attorneys traveling great distances to take depositions, the current practice is for attorneys to offer to pay deponents to come to their offices. An attorney's travel time at an hourly rate can be much more expensive to the client than the cost of a witness's travel expenses alone.

§ 3.18 Strategic Location

After the attorney has determined which locations comport with the discovery rules, he should decide which location affords the greatest strategic advantage. Common sense dictates that the deposition be noticed at a location most convenient for the deposing attorney and the client, and least convenient for the adversary. Yet, such a strategy is not only counter-productive, it is subject to sanction. The court's power to enter a protective order will be used to block a deponent's gross inconvenience or expense. Moreover, Fed.R.Civ.P. 11 provides sanctions for the use of discovery to "needlessly increase the cost of litigation." Thus, while it may be common practice for attorneys to beat impecunious adversaries into submission with burdensome discovery requests, such as a distant deposition, this practice violates the Federal Rules.

Rather than attempt to inconvenience the adversary, therefore, attorneys selecting a site for the deposition should ensure the convenience of their own clients. The deposition location, therefore, should be at a reasonable, and *mutually* agreeable place. Where a deposition of the attorney's client is contemplated for the future, the agreement should include a contingency that the future deposition also take place at a mutually convenient place. The location of a deposition clearly becomes a strategic bargaining tool for the course of discovery.

§ 3.19 The Deposition Site—Local

The deposition should be noticed at a place familiar and comfortable to the deposing attorney. Naturally, the deposing attorney's offices are the best place to depose a witness. When the deposition is at the deposing attorney's office, he can reserve a conference room, meet the court reporter and create a "seating chart" for all the participants before the deponent even arrives. He has ready access to additional files and to the advice of colleagues. He also has the ability to use phones and additional offices without fear of losing confidentiality.

The only negative aspect to deposing a witness in one's own office is the access given the adverse attorneys to that office. In a large case where several firm attorneys work on the matter which is the subject of the deposition, it is not uncommon for the adversary's attorneys to overhear the host firm's unsuspecting attorneys talking freely of the case in the nearby firm library or corridors. Attorneys may leave a revealing file in places where it can be viewed by the adversary's attorneys, an inadvertent disclosure having disastrous consequences. Accordingly, any time a deposition (or any other meeting) is to take place in an office, the entire office must be cautioned that the adversary's attorneys will be present. So long as requisite care is taken, an attorney's own office provides the optimal strategic location for a deposition.

§ 3.20 Deposition Site—Out-of-Town

If the deposition must be taken out-of-town, the deposing attorney should try to use the law offices of an attorney with whom he is familiar. Attorneys often accommodate their out-of-town colleagues by providing conference rooms for deposition. The accommodation is reciprocated in kind. Co-counsel in current or prior cases are likely candidates for this accommodation, as are longstanding colleagues of the firm or frequent referral sources. In order to obtain the possible sources of accommodation, a deposing attorney should circulate an intraoffice memorandum well in advance of the deposition which solicits source names and addresses.

In the unfortunate situation where no law office site out-of-town is available, attorneys frequently hold depositions in a hotel room. If the deposition must be held in a hotel, the deposing attorney should reserve one of the hotel's meeting rooms. The meeting room should contain a telephone, writing materials and beverages. Taking a deposition in a hotel meeting room is vastly superior to taking a deposition in a small hotel room. A deposition taken in a dark, cramped hotel room across twin-beds makes for a great war story, but also makes for a bad deposition. The deposing attorney should insist that the deposition take place in a comfortable, well-supplied and formal room.

§ 3.21   Persons Attending the Deposition

Depositions are not generally considered open proceedings for public attendance. Seattle Times Co. v. Rhinehart, 467 U.S. 20 at 33, 104 S.Ct. 2199 at 2208, 81 L.Ed.2d 17 (1984). The following individuals will be present during the deposition:

(1) *The deponent.* Whether a party, witness or other non-party, any person who has information deemed relevant to the issues in a litigation is subject to deposition. His testimony is likely to provide evidence admissible at the time of trial thereby falling within the acceptable scope of pretrial discovery.

(2) *Attorney representing the deponent.* This attorney, if representing the party or retained by a non-party, has the right to monitor the propriety and direction of the proceedings through the use of objections.

(3) *The examining or deposing attorney.* This attorney represents a party to the litigation and is usually the one who noticed the deposition thereby taking the lead in questioning.

(4) *Other party attorneys.* Any party to the litigation has a right to have an attorney present at every deposition for the purpose of uncovering information relevant to their client's role in the litigation.

(5) *The court reporter.* A certified reporter, or notary public, administers the oath to the deponent and records all testimony in writing for subsequent transcription.

(6) *The parties to the litigation.* Any party has a right to be present at all depositions. The court may exercise discretion to limit the attendance of a party, through a protective order under Fed.R.Civ.P. 26, but it is rare for a judge to prevent a party from attending any deposition. But see Galella v. Onassis, 487 F.2d 986, 997 (2d Cir.1973) where a trial judge excluded the plaintiff photographer from Jacqueline Onassis's deposition. The presence of a party at deposition is a strategic move which can serve to intimidate the deponent; conversely, a party's presence may assist the deponent to recall and state his testimony.

(7) *Third-party attendance.* Whether other persons can attend a deposition is unclear. Fed.R.Civ.P. 26(c)(5) permits the issuance of a protective order so as to permit a deposition to proceed "with no one present except persons designated by the court." *Implied* by the rule is the suggestion that anyone may attend the proceedings unless precluded by protective order.

Protective orders are most likely to be sought against members of the media. Seattle Times Co. v. Rhinehart, 467 U.S. 20, 104 S.Ct. 2199, 81 L.Ed.2d 17 (1984) confirms the court's view of a deposition as less than a public proceeding. Unlike a trial, depositions are set for a time convenient to the attorneys and parties involved; they are not designed to meet the needs of the general public. Reality and practicality dictate that a judge will exercise discretion to restrict attendance by third persons if so requested by one of the attorneys.

Theoretically, there are few instances when a third party needs to be in attendance at a deposition. One clear conflict, however, would be an attorney who wants an expert witness present during the deposition of the opposing party's expert witness. The examiner's own expert can provide information and advice to assist in question development during the deposition; such assistance may be seen by a judge as being beyond the scope of propriety. Nevertheless, absent a protective order, no case law to date specifically restricts the presence of any third party beyond the media. Recall that Fed.R.Civ.P. 26(c)(5) requires a showing of good cause for a protective order to issue. The need to protect a patent or trade secret are examples of when restricting attendance can be desirable.

§ 3.22   Attendance in a Class Action Case

Attorneys taking the depositions of class action plaintiffs should seriously consider obtaining a protective order pursuant to Fed.R.Civ.P. 26(c)(5). While each named class member is a party and hence presumptively able to attend at the others' depositions, such attendance is extremely prejudicial. One key issue in class actions is the commonality of the claims or defenses of the class members. If class members are able to attend each other's deposition, their individual stories will no doubt assume a commonality. The attorney deposing class members should seek and receive a protective order, allowing him to depose each of the named class representatives outside the presence of the other plaintiffs.

§ 3.23   Persons Before Whom Depositions May Be Taken

The process of preparing for a deposition includes the selection of a court reporter or person before whom the deposition may be taken. The person must be both qualified and reliable.

Depositions within the United States may be taken before:

1. an officer authorized by federal law to administer oaths;

2. an officer authorized by the law of the place where the deposition is taken to administer oaths;

3. a person appointed by the court in which the action is pending; or

4. any person provided for by the parties in a written stipulation. *See* Fed.R.Civ.P. 28(a), 29(*l*).

These persons are empowered both to administer oaths and to take testimony.

The person selected to administer oaths and take testimony may, however, be disqualified for interest. The Rules provide that no deposition shall be taken before a person who is:

1. a relative of any party;

2. an employee of any party;

3. an attorney for any party;

4. a relative of an attorney of any party;

5. an employee of an attorney of any party; or

6. financially interested in the action.

See Fed.R.Civ.P. 28(c).

Although the Rules suggest that a court reporter employed by an attorney may be subject to disqualification, they have never been construed so strictly. Attorneys should ensure that the court reporter whom they have chosen has cleared any conflicts check.

Objections to the disqualifying interest of a person before whom the deposition will be taken can be waived. The objection must be made either before the deposition begins or as soon thereafter as the grounds for the objection become known or could be discovered with reasonable diligence. Fed.R.Civ.P. 32(d)(2). Failure to make a seasonable objection constitutes a waiver. Moreover, while the Rule mandates that a deposition not be taken before a person with a disqualifying interest, the parties may agree, by written stipulation, that the deposition be taken before such a person. Fed.R.Civ.P. 29.

In addition to being qualified, the person selected to record the deposition should be reliable. Attorneys should select a familiar, competent, cost-effective reporting service. Most reporting services respond to firm loyalty with group rates or bulk discounts. The loyalty is also rewarded by excellent service and, in some cases, special attention. Such attention is particularly helpful when a transcript is needed on an expedited basis or when extra copies of exhibits are required. Finally, there is some tactical advantage to taking a deposition before a familiar reporter; it may create the impression to the adversary that depositions are a routine part of your practice and expertise.

§ 3.24   Methods of Recording Deposition

A deposition must be recorded. *See* Fed.R.Civ.P. 30(c). Further, it must be recorded by the officer who administers the oath, or someone acting under his direction. Fed.R.Civ.P. 30(c). Leave of court is not required where the deposition is recorded by stenographic means, the typical procedure. A court reporter, who is authorized to administer oaths, also transcribes the oral examination. As a consequence, most depositions result in written transcripts. They record only the audible utterances of the examiner, deponent and attorneys. Naturally, the quality of the record is only as good as the quality of the reporter. Some reporters transcribe every utterance—including verbal pauses such as "uh, um, ah." Others, however, edit such utterances from the final transcript. Still other reporters place their own gloss on the transcription in a well-intentioned effort to have the testimony make sense. But all court reporters will miss a key word or err from time to time. No court reporter can put into writing either the demeanor of the deponent or the non-verbal component of the interaction. Thus, stenography is an imperfect, though familiar, method of recording a deposition.

In keeping with technological advances in recording devices, the Rules permit attorneys to seek a court order that deposition testimony be recorded by other than stenographic means. Fed.R.Civ.P. 30(b)(4). The parties may also stipulate in writing that the deposition be taken by other than stenographic means. *Id.* The order or stipulation must on its face designate:

1. the person before whom the deposition is to be taken;

2. the manner of recording; and

3. the manner of preserving and filing the record. *Id.*

As a general rule, the courts will support the use of experimental methods to record a deposition. *See e.g.,* Colonial Times, Inc. v. Gasch, 509 F.2d 517 (D.C.Cir.1975). Those trial courts preserve their wide discretion to conduct discovery, so a motion seeking an alternative recording method should urge one or more of the following:

1. stenographic means are inadequate or unnecessarily expensive;

2. adequate assurances of the accuracy of the alternative methods exist;

3. the alternative method will be useful at trial, perhaps because the witness will be unavailable.

See e.g., UAW v. National Caucus of Labor Committees, 525 F.2d 323, 326 (2d Cir.1975).

The alternative methods of recording include motion picture, tape recorder and videotape. Moreover, the Federal Rules specifically sanction the taking of a deposition by telephone, Fed. R.Civ.P. 30(b)(7). Videotape is currently the most frequently used alternative to stenography. Videotape records both the audible utterances and the non-verbal cues of the deponent. It can pick up the demeanor of the witness, and can reveal non-verbal cues given to the witness by the examiner or defending attorney. The videotaped deposition has the additional advantage at trial of being less boring to a jury than the reading of page after page of a deposition transcript.

Form 3–1

Timing of Pre–commencement Deposition

Deponent	Deponent's District	Petition Filed	Expected Adverse Parties	Notice Served 20 Days Before Hearing Date on Each Party	Hearing Date	Disposition

Form 3–2

Timing—Plaintiff Deposing Witness Within 30 Days of Serving Complaint

Deponent	Complaint Served	Notices For	Period Expires	Sought Discovery	Notice Served	Statement of Unavailability	Facts Supporting	Rule 11 Signature	Leave Granted

Form 3–3

Timing—Deposition 30 Days After Service of Complaint

Deponent	Complaint Served	30 days Period Expire	Deposition Notice Served	Deposition Noticed for	Deposition Scheduled	Deposition Date	Deposition Time

Form 3–4

Timing—Experts

Expert Deponent	Motion to Take Deposition Filed	Motion Granted	Notes

Form 3–5

Proper Deposition Locations

Deponent	Party or Officer, Director, Managing Agent or Testifying Agent	Notice Non-party	Subpoena Served	Rule 45(d) Served	Residence	Business	Employ	Service	Deposition Locations

Form 3–6

Notice of Deposition to Individual Party

Plaintiff

    v.   No. _____

Defendant

NOTICE OF ORAL DEPOSITION OF _____

PLEASE TAKE NOTICE that the oral deposition of _____ will be taken in accordance with Federal Rule of Civil Procedure 30 [*State Rule of Procedure* _____] at the offices of _____, on _____, 19__, beginning at _____ and continuing from day to day until completion.

The witness is requested to bring to the deposition the documents described on the attached page.

_____

[*Signature*]

Form 3-7

Notice of Oral Deposition of Organization Party

Plaintiff		
	v.	No. _____
Defendant		

NOTICE OF ORAL DEPOSITION OF _____

PLEASE TAKE NOTICE that the oral deposition of _____ will be taken pursuant to Federal Rule of Civil Procedure 30(b)(6) at the offices of _____, on _____, 19__, beginning at _____ and continuing from day to day until completion.

The matters on which the examination is requested include _____

_____

_____ .

In accordance with Fed.R.Civ.P. 30(b)(6), _____ shall designate officers, directors or agents to testify on its behalf as to matters known or reasonably available to _____.

The witness or witnesses designated by _____ shall bring to the deposition the document described on the attached page.

_____
[*Signature*]

Author's Comment

The standards for proper notice to depose a corporate or association party contain additional requirements. Federal Rule of Civil Procedure 30(b)(6) allows the deposing party to name as the deponent a corporation, partnership, governmental agency or other association. In doing so, however, the deposing party should "designate with reasonable particularity matters on which examination is requested." When the deponent is a non-party, this designation is compulsory. The burden then shifts to the named organization to designate persons to testify on its behalf as to matters presumptively within the knowledge of the organization. Fed.R.Civ.P. 30(b)(6). The above form provides sufficient notice for a Rule 30(b)(6) deposition.

Form 3–8

Notice of Oral Deposition by Other Than Stenographic Means

Plaintiff

        v.   No. _____

Defendant

NOTICE OF ORAL DEPOSITION OF _____

PLEASE TAKE NOTICE that the oral deposition of _____ will be taken pursuant to Federal Rule of Civil Procedure 30(b)(6) at the offices of _____, on _____, 19__, beginning at _____ and continuing from day to day until completion.

In accordance with [*the stipulation entered between the parties*] [*court order entered*] on _____, the deposition shall be taken before _____, will be recorded by means of _____, will be presented by _____ and filed by _____.

_____

[*Signature*]

Form 3-9

Deposition Subpoena—Individual

Plaintiff

                           v.   No. _____

Defendant

TO: _____

YOU ARE COMMANDED to appear at: _____ on _____ at _____ to testify at the taking of a deposition in the above action pending in the United States District Court for the _____, and to produce at the deposition the documents listed on the attached page.

Dated _____, 19__.

By _____
District Clerk

Form 3-10

Deposition Subpoena—Organization

Plaintiff

        v.   No. _____

Defendant

TO: _____

YOU ARE COMMANDED to appear at: _____ on _____ at _____ to testify at the taking of a deposition in the above action pending in the United States District Court for the _____, and to produce at the deposition the documents listed on the attached page.

Pursuant to Federal Rule of Civil Procedure 30(b)(6), _____ shall file a designation with the court specifying one or more officers, directors, agents to testify regarding matters known or reasonably known to _____.

Dated _____, 19__.

By _____

District Clerk

Motion for Commission

Plaintiff

               v.   No. _____

Defendant

MOTION FOR COMMISSION TO TAKE DEPOSITION OF _____

NOW COMES _____ and moves this court to enter an order granting a commission to take the deposition of _____ who resides in _____. In support of its motion, _____ states:

1. The witness, _____, knows facts relevant to this case.

2. The court reporter to whom the commission should be issued is _____, so that that court reporter may issue a subpoena to assure the appearance of the witness.

3. No undue prejudice to any party or witness will result from the issuance of the commission.

WHEREFORE, _____ respectfully requests this court to enter an order granting a commission in this action.

Respectfully Submitted

By _____
[*Signature*]

[NOTICE OF MOTION]

[CERTIFICATION OF SERVICE]

Motion for Commission for Foreign Deposition

Plaintiff		
	v.	No. _____
Defendant		

MOTION FOR A COMMISSION TO TAKE FOREIGN DEPOSITION

NOW COMES _____ and moves this court to enter an order granting a commission to take the deposition of _____, a citizen of _____. In support of its motion, _____ states as follows:

1. The above matter which is pending in the United States district court for the _____ district of _____, arises, out of _____.

2. The proposed witness, _____ who resides at _____, will provide significant evidence to be used in the pending litigation, because _____.

WHEREFORE, _____ respectfully requests this court to enter an order granting a commission authorizing _____, who resides at _____ and is qualified to accept the commission to take the deposition of _____ at _____ on _____.

Respectfully Submitted

By _____

[*Signature*]

Letters Rogatory

Plaintiff

v.   No. _____

Defendant

APPLICATION FOR LETTERS OF REQUEST

NOW COMES _____ and submits this application pursuant to Federal Rule of Civil Procedure 28(b) for a Letter Rogatory. In support of its application, _____ states:

1. This case which involves Plaintiff _____ and Defendant _____, arises out of the following: _____

_____

_____.

2. A Letter of Request is necessary to obtain the deposition of _____, a citizen of _____.

3. The deposition of _____ will produce significant evidence to be used in an action pending [to be commenced] because: _____

_____.

4. The deponent will be examined regarding the following matters: _____

_____.

5. In addition, the witness is requested to bring to deposition the documents described on the attached page, which are in his possession, custody and control, and which will used in this matter.

WHEREFORE, _____ respectfully requests this court to issue a Letter Rogatory to _____ for the purpose of taking the deposition of _____, at _____, on _____.

Respectfully Submitted

By _____
   [*Signature*]

Form 3–14

Deposition Site

Deponent	Proper Locations	Optimal Locations	Intra-Office Memo Sent	Possible Site	Deposition Site

Chapter 4

PRE–DEPOSITION PROCEDURES

Table of Sections

---

§ 4.1 The Ritualistic Nature of Depositions

The beginning of depositions tend to be ritualistic. Most attorneys begin the ritual by doing one or more of the following: introducing themselves to the deponent, offering the attendees coffee, soft drinks or water, reminding the deponent that he will be under oath, describing the deposition procedure to the deponent, and inquiring whether the deponent is experiencing any physical or psychological difficulties which would warrant postponing the deposition. The ritual serves to put the deponent at ease and establishes a cooperative atmosphere.

§ 4.2 Non–verbal Communication in the Deposition

The manner in which a message is delivered is often more potent than the message conveyed. The transcribed deposition record will not reflect tone of voice or mannerisms, so it is important for the examiner to know how to place both visual and auditory cues properly into the record. Nonverbal factors affecting the deposition include both the set-up of the deposition room which creates the atmosphere for the interaction, and the monitoring and exercise of other nonverbal cues during the course of the interaction itself, *see* Form 4–1.

§ 4.3 Non–verbal Communication in the Deposition—Physical Layout of Deposition Room

The seating arrangement in the deposition affects the manner in which the interaction plays out. The examiner is best advised to place his back toward the door. The deponent should be seated directly across from the examiner. *See* Lewis, Effective Use of Discovery Tools, 52 Okla.Bar J. 1773, 1776 (1981). The psychological advantage of placing the examiner between the deponent and the door is the creation of pressure on the deponent that he may not leave until all information desired is obtained. Sitting across from the deponent also produces the pressure of direct eye contact. The court reporter is best placed to one side of the deponent, facing the examining attorney. This arrangement allows the court reporter to hear the two main conversants and makes it easier to hand exhibits between the reporter and the deponent. Under this arrangement, the deponent's attorney sits on the other side of the deponent, thereby facing the examiner and establishing his role as defender.

Where the presenting attorney is known to consistently obstruct the deposition, the examiner may modify the seating arrangement by putting the defending attorney next to the court reporter. Since the court reporter can overhear comments or witness coaching, these comments may make it into the record thereby deterring the attorney from such obstructionist tactics.

The examiner should even give thought to the size of the conference room and table. A narrow table creates pressure on the deponent but a larger table permits privacy to confer extensively with colleagues or consult notes.

Proper lighting in the room is essential for effective note taking. Comfortable chairs are imperative for a lengthy deposition. An examiner who wishes a deposition to move swiftly or be short in length can modify these arrangements. He may provide uncomfortable chairs or refuse to offer amenities such as coffee or water, leading everyone to move through the questioning as quickly as possible.

§ 4.4 Non–verbal Communication in the Deposition—Monitoring Non–verbal Cues

Aside from the room set up and orientation or angle at which people sit in relation to one another, posture plays a key role at the deposition table. A person who desires to take charge of the situation will often sit upright, and positioned in the center of the other participants. This face-to-face confrontation ensures attention and controls intimidation. Maintaining eye contact along with facial expression is an important non-verbal factor, as frequent eye blinking, for example, can denote puzzlement or disbelief. Prolonged eye contact arouses uneasiness in the deponent and may compel the deponent to elaborate on a response. Deponents who are embarrassed or otherwise uncomfortable will avoid eye contact and shift their gaze away from the examiner.

The examiner should monitor the deponent's non-verbal responses. Crossed arms may indicate defiance or lack of openness; rapid eye movement, expanded pupils, perspiration, frequent leg crossing and wringing, tapping hands and fingers and a tightened jaw and crocodile grin suggest anxiety.

Posture also varies with emotional state. Depression is often reflected in stooped shoulders or a sagging back. Speech irregularities, such as hesitancy or stuttering, may reflect repression or anxiety.

Many non-verbal cues are difficult to read both because people learn how to mask their feelings and because a gesture can have more than one meaning. Such difficulty presents itself when attempting to uncover whether a deponent is telling the truth. Generally, an asymmetrical smile is false, as when synchronization is absent between gesture and facial expression. Expressive people tend to slow down their movements when they lie, becoming unusually composed and making fewer gestures. Good liars often have trouble with the onset, duration and release of facial expression. While in fear, both eyebrows are raised and unconsciously pulled together; in anger, a narrow tightening of the lips can be noted. A smile that lingers beyond four or five seconds, may reveal an attempt to deceive. No examiner should read anyone's signal as indicating what the deponent is really thinking; a constant monitoring of cues may in their entirety provide a more reliable reading of the deponent's frame of mind.

§ 4.5 Putting Non–verbal Cues on the Record

Whether the examiner wishes to put on the record the deponent's conduct will be a strategic decision made at the time. Where a deponent is intentionally evasive or hostile, placing such cues on the record may be strategically important to letting the deponent know these tactics do not go unnoticed. More effectively, however, a deponent who is seemingly evasive or unresponsive out of nervousness or uncertainty should be encouraged to relax and reminded that so long as the truth is told, the deponent should be confident and comfortable.

In the latter case, the intimidation created by making a record is avoided in favor of a supportive measure.

§ 4.6 Assisting the Court Reporter

The examiner must recognize the important role played by the court reporter. The reporter records all testimony and objections which occur during the deposition. In order to reduce the possibility of transcript errors during the deposition, the reporter should be made as comfortable as possible. The examiner can assist the reporter by providing prior to the deposition a caption of the case, spellings of difficult names or terms to be used during the deposition and a copy of anything likely to be read into the record. Breaks should be taken every 60 to 90 minutes not only to permit the deponent and participants to relax and re-gather thoughts, but also to allow the court reporter to rejuvenate his or her own energies. *See* Form 4–1.

Maintaining a proper professional relationship with the court reporter can result in a more complete transcript. Excellent reporters will, on their own initiative, "clean up the transcript" by eliminating false starts of the attorney or non-question cluttering such as "I see", "o.k." or repetition of responses. If an attorney wishes these types of phrases to appear on the record, they should request the court reporter to transcribe the interaction verbatim without any editorial clean-up. Court reporters are, of course, human and will tend to assist those attorneys who treat them well. For example, deponents who give a non-verbal response such as "uh huh" may be requested by the court reporter to state a verbal response, if the examiner forgets to do so. Other reporters will do nothing unless specifically requested by an attorney. Antagonizing the reporter will discourage him or her from providing such procedural assistance. As officers of the court, the reporter has the obligation to ensure an accurate and complete transcription of the interaction, but responsibilities get exercised differently by different reporters; their view of their own role will vary as well. As a result, attorneys are best advised to maintain good relations with the court reporter.

§ 4.7 Agreeing to "the Usual Stipulations"

It is not uncommon after the introductory amenities, for a court reporter or the presenting attorney to ask whether all parties present will agree to "the usual stipulations." Some attorneys readily agree to these stipulations; most attorneys do not know what these stipulations are to which they have just agreed. The examiner should request that any stipulation be specified onto the record.

Following is a list of potential stipulations:

(1) Agreement that the deposition will be taken pursuant to "Rules of Civil Procedure." This stipulation is superfluous because all applicable civil procedural and court rules govern the interaction whether or not the attorneys agree that they do so. Attorneys may not agree to waive any governing deposition rules. Thus, there is little purpose in making the stipulation.

(2) Agreement to waive the oath. There is purpose in an attempt to waive the oath. Whether the deposition is used as an impeachment tool at trial or is to be read into evidence at trial, it is imperative that the testimony be given under oath. It would be catastrophic for the deponent to be asked at trial: "and you were sworn to tell the truth at the deposition, weren't you?" with the answer: "no, I recall the attorneys agreeing to waive the oath, so I was not sworn." The examining attorney must ensure that all deponents explicitly take an oath on the record.

(3) Agree to waive the reading and signing of the deposition transcript. This stipulation should rarely be entered into. The reporter's duties are difficult and often tedious; the likelihood of error at some point is always present. Attorneys should expend the time it takes to read and ensure the accuracy of the deposition transcript. The parties may, however, agree that the transcript be signed before any notary. This agreement is useful when the deponent lives at a great distance from the deposition site and it would be inconvenient for that person

to sign the transcript in the presence of a particular court reporter. *See* Blumenkopf, Deposition Strategy and Tactics, 5 Am.J.Tr.Adv. 231, 239 (1981).

(4) Agree that withdrawn questions will be omitted from the transcript. This stipulation creates a cleaner record, and saves transcription costs. In addition, it benefits the examining attorney because any unpreparedness, confusion, or strategy inherent in such comments gets eliminated from the transcript.

(5) Agreement that all evidentiary objections will be preserved until trial. Such an agreement may be invalid under Fed.R.Civ.P. 32 since the Rule requires that "errors and irregularities occurring at the oral examination . . . in the form of the question . . . are waived unless seasonable objection thereto is made at the taking of the deposition." The Rule's language is mandatory; any stipulation to the contrary could be deemed invalid at trial. In that circumstance, the failure to object to the form of a question at deposition will constitute a waiver of the objection at trial.

(6) Agreement that any opposing attorney's objection inures to the benefit of all. This stipulation precludes other attorneys from having to make the same objection on the record. The stipulation results in fewer and shorter interruptions, thereby benefiting the examining attorney.

(7) Agreement that an instruction from counsel that the deponent not answer shall be deemed the equivalent of the deponent's refusal to answer. Such a stipulation saves time by eliminating the necessary steps to certifying the question. However, where a deponent seems independent or does not otherwise act in conjunction with his attorney, such a stipulation should be strategically avoided as many answers may likely be gained in the face of contrary advice from the defending attorney.

§ 4.8 The Procedural Rules

The examiner routinely begins the deposition by stating a series of rules which establish a framework for the interaction. These rules keep the court reporter's record clear and establish proper decorum during the deposition. Most examining attorneys state some or all of these rules in a drone or matter-of-fact tone of voice. By so doing, the examiner gives up an important opportunity to establish his or her own credibility for the deponent. Rather, the attorney should state each of the following rules in question form to ensure the deponent's understanding and adherence to each of them. Explicit understanding established on the record will be useful should the transcript need to be used to impeach during trial.

Some defending attorneys will interrupt the reading of the rules by noting that they properly prepared the deponent and informed him of the rules. When confronted with this tactic, the examiner should persist in stating the rules to both maintain control of the deposition and establish, on the record, the deponent's understanding of the following rules:

(1) I'm going to ask you a series of questions regarding the incident that is the subject of this lawsuit and which occurred on _____. Do you understand this?

(2) If at any time you don't understand one of my questions, please say so and I will repeat or rephrase it until you do understand the question. Do you understand this rule?

(3) If at any time you don't hear one of my questions, please say so and I will repeat it to ensure that you do hear it. Do you understand?

(4) All of your answers must be verbal since the court reporter cannot take down non-verbal cues such as a nod of the head or shrug of the shoulders. Do you understand that all your responses must be stated in words? [Many deponents will answer this question with an "uh huh" which should then be followed by clarifying that they have just violated the rule.]

(5) If you do not know the answer to a question, simply state you do not know. I do not expect you to guess or to speculate as to responses. Do you understand?

(6) Please make your answers clear for the record so the court reporter can accurately transcribe each of the words you state. Do you understand this?

(7) Please wait until I finish each of my questions before answering and I will wait until you finish each of your answers before I ask another question. In this way the court reporter keeps a clear record without interruption. Do you understand?

(8) We will take a break about every hour to give the court reporter and all of us a chance to refresh ourselves. If you need a break prior to that time, please request one and we will take one. Do you understand?

(9) You understand that the deposition will be transcribed by the court reporter and that everything said here today will be recorded. Do you understand that?

(10) You understand that, at trial, all the testimony given here today will be available in written form, and if I ask you a question at trial that I ask you today, you may be asked to explain or otherwise account for any difference in your answers that may occur. Do you understand?

(11) You understand that your testimony today is being given under oath, as if you were in a court of law, *i.e.,* you have been sworn to tell the truth and if you fail to do so adverse consequences could result. Do you understand?

(12) And finally, the deponent must be asked the catch-all question: Do you understand each and every one of these rules as I have stated them? If the deponent answers in the negative, the examiner must take the time to uncover which rule was unclear and review that rule with the deponent. If the deponent answers in the affirmative, the examiner should follow up with this final statement: "That's fine. You understand that these rules assure that if I ask a question and you give an answer to that question it will be assumed that you understood the question as posed and your answer is intended to be responsive as rendered. Do you understand this statement?" This final affirmation fairly precludes any claim at trial by the deponent that a question was confusing or an answer was not responsive due to a poorly phrased question.

The recitation of these rules establishes both attorney tone and control. If a cordial relationship is desired, these initial remarks should be stated in a friendly manner. A more stern, formal atmosphere necessitates a more rigid recitation of the rules. Deponents respond to the atmosphere created by the examiner during these initial moments. Thus, the rules are an integral part of an effective deposition, and should be stated with meaning.

§ 4.9 Use of Exhibits

Whenever possible, the examining attorney should have exhibits organized and marked for use prior to the deposition. *See* Form 4–2. The ritual of having the court reporter mark the deposition during the interaction, though archaic, is generally employed. An attorney can mark each exhibit with the name of the deponent, date of the deposition and number of the exhibit (ordered in some sequential fashion) as part of effective planning. Exhibits are marked to keep the record clear. The attorney should remember that statements such as "Let the record reflect the deponent has marked the photograph" leave ambiguity as to which photograph, what was marked, and where the photograph was marked. All markings made on an exhibit or reference made to the exhibit should be made clearly, leaving no ambiguity on the record. Attaching to the deposition transcript a copy of each exhibit eliminates potential confusion over which exhibit was used in the deposition. Certainly the record will be confused if an exhibit is not described in a fashion which distinguishes it from other exhibits.

Whether marked before or during the deposition, the examiner should describe the exhibit at least once on the record. For example:

ATTORNEY: Court reporter, kindly mark as Mr. Jones' Exhibit No. 1 this three inch by five inch photograph, depicting the front of the post office and date stamped July 29, 1988.

The examiner, out of professional courtesy, should show the exhibit to opposing counsel so that all attorneys are knowledgeable of the exhibit being discussed.

Introducing an exhibit in a deposition is not fraught with the technicalities of "offering" that exhibit into evidence at trial. At deposition, the exhibit automatically becomes part of the record; objections are for trial. There is also no need to lay a foundation for questioning a deponent about an exhibit, unless the deposition is to be read into evidence at trial for an unavailable witness; thus, establishing foundation can prevent subsequent admission problems at a trial.

Form 4–1

Monitoring Non-verbal Cues

Case Name _____

Deposition of _____

Date _____

1. Desired Atmosphere (cordial, hostile, cooperative):

   _____

   _____

   _____

   _____

2. Deposition Room Set–Up to Meet Desired Atmosphere:

   A. Room Set–Up: _____

      _____

      _____

   B. Lighting: _____

      _____

      _____

   C. Seating Arrangement (can diagram):

   D. Refreshments to be offered, if any:

      _____

      _____

      _____

3. Assisting the Court Reporter

   Check off to insure compliance with each:

   A. Provided caption   _____

   B. Provide spelling of terms/names   _____

   C. Offer breaks   _____

Organization of Exhibits

Case _____   File No. _____

Date of Deposition _____   Deponent _____

Issue: _____

Question	Document Needed–Title	Cite	Exhibit No.

Issue: _____

Question	Document Needed–Title	Cite	Exhibit No.

Issue: _____

Question	Document Needed–Title	Cite	Exhibit No.

Part II

THE DEPOSING ATTORNEY'S PERSPECTIVE

Chapter 5

EFFECTIVE DEPOSITION QUESTIONING

Table of Sections

---

§ 5.1 Availability of Leading Questions

Most deponents are warned by their attorneys not to volunteer information or otherwise assist the examiner in the deposition. The examiner must therefore be prepared to elicit information strategically and carefully. There are a series of questioning techniques available to examiners; selecting the desirable technique will depend upon the phase of the deposition.

Deposing a person aligned with the opposition permits the examiner the right to lead, or create the flavor of a cross-examination. Whenever a party deposes a hostile witness, an adverse party or a witness identified with an adverse party, the interrogation may proceed by leading questions in accordance with Fed.R.Ev. 611(c). While the examiner has the right to lead, he may choose not to do so depending on the purpose of his question or the area of inquiry. For example, when the examiner's central purpose is to gather information, the use of leading questions will be limited. Conversely, when the examiner wishes to pin down certain testimony, leading questions provide the same control as cross-examination at trial. The fundamental rule that a deposition may operate like a cross examination is one not often remembered or employed by most examining attorneys. In fact, many examiners retreat from an objection by opposing counsel to the use of leading questions. Examiners simply need to remember their right to use leading questions during depositions. The type of question used will vary with the phase of the deposition.

§ 5.2   Areas of Inquiry

The examiner typically inquires into three areas: the background of the deponent, the cause of action and the injury or damages (past, present and future) incurred. This outline represents the usual order in which questioning is conducted, but no rule precludes an examining attorney from modifying the order or beginning at any desired point. In fact, beginning a deposition at a key or crucial fact-issue can take the other participants off guard thereby preventing them from responding with a carefully designed answer created prior to the deposition. The examiner's central objective is to exhaust the witness's knowledge about the facts in the case. For this reason, a checklist approach to depositions is not recommended. There are a variety of checklist sources on the market, but the attorney who scripts the interaction risks the loss of effective follow-up and probing which follows in the interaction, not on a checklist. Form 5–1 provides an alternative and rather unique means of preparing for questioning. By creating a question tree, the attorney uses logic and follow-up to pursue each potential answer given by a deponent. The deposition retains flexibility but also issues completeness as each branch of the question tree, for any particular issue, is followed up.

§ 5.3   Background of Deponent

It is important to understand the deponent's general background and personal history. Understanding where the deponent currently lives and has lived provides information on his attitudes and desires as well as essential contact information. The attorney may wish to speak to neighbors or housemates regarding the deponent. Gathering information regarding a deponent's educational and employment background provides insight into his level of intelligence, sophistication and credibility. Information regarding the deponent's age, marital status and family history reflects the likely image of the deponent in the jurors' minds. The background of a party deponent provides information useful in subsequent jury selection; knowing the deponent's background provides a better basis for an educated selection of jurors who will likely identify with, or not identify with, that deponent.

§ 5.4   Cause of Action

Gathering information about the cause of action will highlight the strengths of the deponent's story and signal necessary defenses. The manner of questioning will depend on the approach chosen by the examiner, but the ultimate facts which reflect the legal issues must be investigated thoroughly. *See* Form 5–1. For example, the components in a tort case include proximate cause, standard of care, and breach of duty, each of which must be an area of inquiry. In addition, all of the complementary or evidentiary facts which may prove or disprove each of the ultimate facts must be investigated. Facts which weaken the deponent's position must be gathered to reduce the credibility of the deponent or the weight of the testimony in the event of trial or to posture for settlement.

§ 5.5   Damages

Damages or injuries represent a separate and major area of inquiry. Investigating all past, present and future damages is essential regardless of the position taken with regard to liability in the case. Moreover, the extent of damages impacts the value of potential settlement and helps determine verdict exposure.

§ 5.6 Question Format—Open vs. Closed Questions

The examiner should decide to use general, open-ended questions which elicit narrative answers, close-ended questions that clarify and probe, or a combination of both. As a rule, the examiner should begin with general inquiries and then shift to specific probes. It is easier for a deponent to first explain generalities, and then to clarify specifics.

So long as the examiner proceeds logically, he may shift the subject matter of the questions frequently and suddenly. This tactic limits the deponent's ability to give a planned answer when such a question is asked out of anticipated sequence. The use of open-ended questions permits the deponent to narrate answers freely and are quite useful unless the deponent rambles. The examiner structures responses by explaining or instructing the deponent to answer open-ended questions such as "tell me everything that you said to him and he said to you in that conversation."

§ 5.7 Impeachment Information

The examiner may possess certain impeaching facts which he may wish to consider raising in the deposition. The examiner may wish to save the impeaching ammunition for trial, or disclose the information to intimidate an evasive witness into giving more truthful and complete answers. Raising impeaching information often leads a deponent to believe that the examiner knows more about the case than he admits, leading the deponent to be honest. Raising impeachment information can also motivate the deponent and other attorneys to settle the litigation.

§ 5.8 Estimating Distance and Time

Deponents are often hesitant to estimate distance and time. The examiner can deal with this issue in one of two ways:

1. If the examiner seeks information regarding distance and the deponent states that he is poor at estimating distance, the examiner may begin with extremely high estimates and ask the deponent in sequence whether the distance was greater or less than the exaggerated estimate. This technique locks the deponent into an estimate range.

2. The examiner may ask the deponent to specify the terms in which he would feel comfortable establishing an estimation. For example, some deponents cannot speak in feet but prefer to talk in terms of yards or car lengths. While estimating time or distance is a difficult concept, in general, the examiner can uncover a means by which the deponent will be able to render an estimate, at least in his own terms.

§ 5.9 Closing Questions

The use of closing questions is important to specify the who, what, when, where, why and how questions. It is these components that produce detailed information necessary to complete each component of the deponent's story. Closing questions can clamp off an area: "Have you told us absolutely everything that you remember happening at that time?" or: "Do you remember anything else at all in response to this question?" The examiner should get all details of any conversations held with the deponent including exact quotations or, at a minimum, paraphrases of the conversation.

§ 5.10 Information From Other Sources

Information obtained from a source other than the deponent can be presented in the deposition for verification or contradiction. The deponent who senses a question based on outsider information must exercise caution, since he knows there is an additional source of information. The examiner is advised to first seek the deponent's version through narrative or otherwise neutral questions, before bringing in outside information. When the examiner seeks to influence the deponent's response, the outside information can be presented in a suggestive or leading format.

Examiners are also encouraged to inquire into the feelings, emotions, opinions, thoughts and attitudes of the deponent. Thus, the deposition goes beyond factual information and into complementary aspects of thought or attitude. In this way, the examiner gains a better understanding of how the deponent's mind was operating in relation to the factual scenario.

§ 5.11 Examiner Reaction

The examiner may react to testimony given by a deponent. When an examiner is confused by a deponent's answer, he may suggest the deponent may be in error, or may summarize the testimony to ensure accuracy. When the deponent's answer constitutes an admission, the examiner must decide whether to pursue additional probing which may cause a retraction of the admission. Where the deponent appears to be lying, the examiner may illustrate disbelief or disgust with questions such as: "Are you certain of that response?" which should trigger anxiety in the deponent. A witness who acts in a negative, aggressive or hostile manner is probably best confronted by the attorney on the record. The examiner asks the deponent to cooperate so the deposition can proceed smoothly.

§ 5.12 The Importance of Follow-Up Questions

Although the interaction rules specify that deponents should request clarification of an unclear question, the effective examiner will nevertheless monitor himself to ensure that his questions are simple and clear. *See* Form 5–2. It makes sense to subdivide a question to better obtain an answer which is responsive. For example, an attorney who asks "You saw the witness and approached her?" Answer: "Yes." The record will be ambiguous as to whether the deponent both first saw the witness *and* approached her, or that the deponent approached the witness, *or* was first to see the witness. The examiner must probe, follow-up, and maintain an inquisitive attitude throughout the deposition. As a rule, the deposition is the time to uncover any and all information, whether or not it proves to be damaging.

Where information is uncovered which may be damaging, the examiner is best advised not to react visibly, but to maintain a neutral "poker face." While case position may be shattered or unexpected follow-up work necessary, it is best for case posture for the examiner not to reveal surprise or dismay. After all, any and all facts are likely to be brought out in trial testimony. Always follow-up each fact uncovered by asking: "how do you know?" Where a witness specifies they do not know the answer to a question, always inquire: "who would know?" Such follow-up permits future depositions to be scheduled to obtain the necessary information.

§ 5.13 Deponent Answers—Generally

The examiner must monitor and control the witness and his responses to ensure accuracy and completeness. *See* Form 5–3.

§ 5.14 Unresponsive Answer

Where an answer is unresponsive, the examiner should insist that the witness restate the answer until it is complete and accurate. This may result in the deponent changing his answer to "I don't know," which may have been the truth in the first place. Oftentimes, a deponent's response is off the mark because he resorts to speculation. The follow-up ensures whether that deponent knows something first-hand which would respond directly to the question.

§ 5.15 Rambling Answer

When the deponent rambles, the examiner may either move to strike that portion of the answer which is unresponsive or inform the deponent that he has answered the question. Where the deponent's testimony rambles but is favorable, the record nevertheless needs to be clarified: the examiner can restate and summarize the favorable testimony on the record and then confirm with the deponent that the summary is accurate.

§ 5.16 Incomplete Answer

Where the answer is incomplete, insist that the deponent give a complete and sufficient answer. Ask the deponent whether he knows anything else or inquire whether the deponent has stated everything he knows in full response to the question.

§ 5.17 Handling Objections Made as Strategy

Every non-examining attorney has a right to make an objection during the deposition. Ordinarily, the examiner will insist on an answer to the question, subject to the objection. Fed.R.Civ.P. 30(c).

The examiner should monitor whether objections begin to interfere with the direction and goals of the deposition. Where an objecting attorney fails to specify grounds for the objection, and the examiner is uncertain of its basis, a request for explanation should be made on the record. An objection to a poorly phrased question gives the examiner an option to rephrase, withdraw or repeat the question. Often, an objection to relevance can be cured through rephrasing or asking other questions which establish a foundation. Even if the examiner chooses not to modify the question, he is nevertheless entitled to an answer to the question. Fed.R.Civ.P. 32(d)(3)(A). Objections based on any other ground may be "ignored" by the examiner who continues his request for a response from the deponent. Where the deponent appears unsure of how to proceed, the examiner should request the deponent to respond to the question, with the objection being handled by the lawyers at a later date.

Where the defending attorney instructs the deponent not to answer the question, the examiner should request the deponent to state his refusal to answer on the record (except where there has been a stipulation on this issue). The question should be certified on the record, which preserves the option of having the judge compel an answer. The transcript must clearly reflect the question not answered, the objection, and the instruction not to answer. Insufficient reasons for the objection may produce sanctions pursuant to Fed.R.Civ.P. 37, including costs rendered against the objecting attorney.

Where an attorney constantly imposes objections, he may do so as strategic interference with the interaction. The examiner may cooperatively remind the objector that most substantive objections are preserved for trial, there being no need to continue rendering objections. If a situation gets intolerable, the examiner may terminate the deposition to obtain a protective order or Fed.R.Civ.P. 37 sanction.

The examiner must maintain control of the deposition. Where attorneys interfere with the direction of the deposition, the examiner must insist that the deposition proceed in his selected manner and direction. Where hostile discussions ensue, the examiner is best advised to keep all discussion on the record, including offensive non-verbal conduct. For example, specifying on the record that the defending attorney "need not pound your fist on the table and scream at a high pitch" records for a judge the requisite conduct to render sanctions against the offending attorney. A request for a recess may calm the participants, but may, like the objection, disrupt an excellent flow of an examiner's questions. Essentially, the examiner should monitor whether interferences are being made on a legitimate basis, or simply to interrupt the "effective roll" of the examiner; in the latter instance, the examiner is best advised to proceed after warning all other participants to respect the proper decorum of the proceedings.

§ 5.18 Requests for Recess

The defending attorney has the right to confer with his deponent during the questioning or during recess. Where the defending attorney passes the deponent a note for a conference, such conduct should be placed on the record by the examiner. Courts recognize the attorney's right to initiate a private conference for the purpose of determining whether a privilege should be asserted (see Standing Order 13 on Effective Discovery in Civil Cases, 102 F.R.D. 351 (E.D. N.Y.)), but some attorneys abuse this procedure by using private conferences to coach the deponent on responses.

Where a conference between a non-party deponent and an attorney occurs during a recess, the examiner should question the non-party deponent about the substance of the conference (as such is not protected by any privilege). Where the deponent is a party, the fact that a conversation occurred is not privileged even though the contents may be. The examiner can ask the deponent whether he wishes to change any testimony given before the recess as a result of his conference. Clearly, a changed response will likely appear at trial as the product of attorney prompting during the recess conference.

§ 5.19 Concluding the Deposition

The conclusion of a deposition often is as ritualistic as the opening. The examiner should solidify the testimony given by the deponent and specify any future commitments from that deponent. Verification questions such as: "Have you understood all the questions you answered?" or "Did you reveal all the facts that you were asked about?" serve as sufficient wrap-up. The deponent may be asked to confirm that he answered all questions truthfully and whether or not he wishes to change any answers prior to concluding the deposition. Such questions tighten the transcript and strengthen this tool for impeachment at trial. Some examiners advise the deponent that he has an obligation to supplement any answers given during the deposition should he recall additional information at a later date. Whether supplementation is mandatory under Fed.R.Civ.P. 26(e) is unclear; under the rule the defending attorney may interrupt this request to suggest that he will advise his client appropriately.

§ 5.20 Subsequent Production of Documents

The examiner should specify on the record any agreement or request production of exhibits or other documents previously requested but not produced prior to the deposition. The proceeding is stated to remain "open" for reconvening only regarding such documents. For example, examiner states: "Let the record reflect that [counsel] Mr. Jones has agreed to provide copies of the inspection report and that these records will be provided within seven days at my cost. The deposition may be reconvened at that time for the sole purpose of questioning this deponent with regard to those documents."

Documents not previously produced due to a claimed privilege are subject to questioning to investigate the refusal to turn the document over. In this way, a claim regarding relevancy or work product might be overcome requiring the documents to be turned over subsequently.

A deponent's diary in a personal injury suit is a common subject of such questioning. The existence of a diary is often claimed to be irrelevant prior to the time of the accident in question and work product subsequent to the time of the accident. An examiner's questions which indicate the deponent maintained a diary at his own discretion and not for the purpose of litigation may require the diary to be turned over for inspection. Failure to inquire at the time of deposition could preclude later review. Recapping the request to turn over any such document after the deposition saves time and effort to reconfirm the request in writing.

§ 5.21 Questioning by Other Attorneys

After the lead examiner has completed his questioning, all other attorneys present are permitted to examine the deponent. Fed.R.Civ.P. 30(c). No such examination should occur until the lead examiner has completed his or her questioning.

§ 5.22 Post-deposition Demeanor of Deponent

Once the deposition concludes and the parties take their leave, it is useful to continue observing the demeanor of the deponent and his interaction with his attorney; interesting non-verbal cues are often noted which reflect whether the seemingly injured deponent is really exhausted, uncomfortable perhaps for divulging too much truth, or smirking for feeling he has done a fine job.

§ 5.23 Special Considerations—Deposing the Expert

While all of the procedural rules and considerations specified are applicable to depositions of both lay and expert witnesses, there are specific considerations for expert witnesses. While the factual expert witness testifies much like any other factual witness, the opinion expert witness renders opinions and underlying reasoning. These opinion experts need be examined regarding the specific areas of expertise they possess. Specifically, opinion experts need to be questioned about the following: (1) qualifications as an expert: education, experience, certifications and licenses, publications, speaking experiences, past work as an expert, awards and honors; (2) opinions relative to the litigation; (3) supporting reasons or basis of opinions; (4) sources of information relied upon for opinions; (5) fee structure; (6) expectation regarding testifying at the time of trial; (7) the degree of probability of the rendered opinions; and (8) familiarity with any relevant treatises or other scholarly work. Oftentimes, questioning regarding the experts can be short-circuited at deposition by marking his curriculum vitae as an exhibit and attaching it to the transcript. The examiner should, nevertheless, inquire into relevant background or qualifications which seem broad or unrelated to the litigation.

The examiner must take into account whether the expert is primarily a plaintiff or defense witness in his previous experience. In addition, the examiner should do his homework to uncover whether the information, tests or sources of information relied upon by the expert are sufficient as related to the litigation and whether there are contrary causes or explanations not presented by the adversary's expert.

§ 5.24 Pre-deposition Preparation for Experts

Many examining attorneys use the deposition of the adversary's expert as a time to be educated. Expert depositions should never be taken for this purpose; rather the examiner should be well prepared by his own expert and should conduct sufficient research to be capable of gathering and probing the testimony. Simultaneously, the examiner must not express all his knowledge or he may likely place his own case strategy on the table for the opposing expert to later consider and destroy. Certainly, an appropriate response will be developed by the adversarial expert by the time of the trial. The examiner must therefore create a balance between gathering information, testing the position of the opposing expert, and yet disclosing only that information necessary to conduct effective questioning.

Clearly, the examining attorney seeks sufficient information to prepare for cross examination of that expert at trial. An expert may not testify to matters outside his realm of knowledge and expertise, need not respond to hypotheticals or opinion questions not based on facts in the case, and should not extend beyond his expert's preparation and work for the case at issue.

§ 5.25 Demeanor of Expert

Most experienced experts understand the strategies and techniques of depositions. They are trained to be brief in response, answering only the questions asked. The examiner should not expect the expert to ramble or volunteer any information. Whether or not the expert appears controlled at the time of deposition is likely a planned performance. It is likely that the experienced expert will convey information effectively to a jury in the courtroom. Thus, comments regarding the expert's demeanor at deposition are important to the deposition summary, but should subsequently be modified after the expert's performance at trial since the attorney will likely meet the expert in future cases.

Form 5–1

Question Tree

Case _____   File No. _____

Date of Deposition _____   Deponent _____

Area of Inquiry: <u>Background</u>

Issue: _____

Question # 1 (Q1):

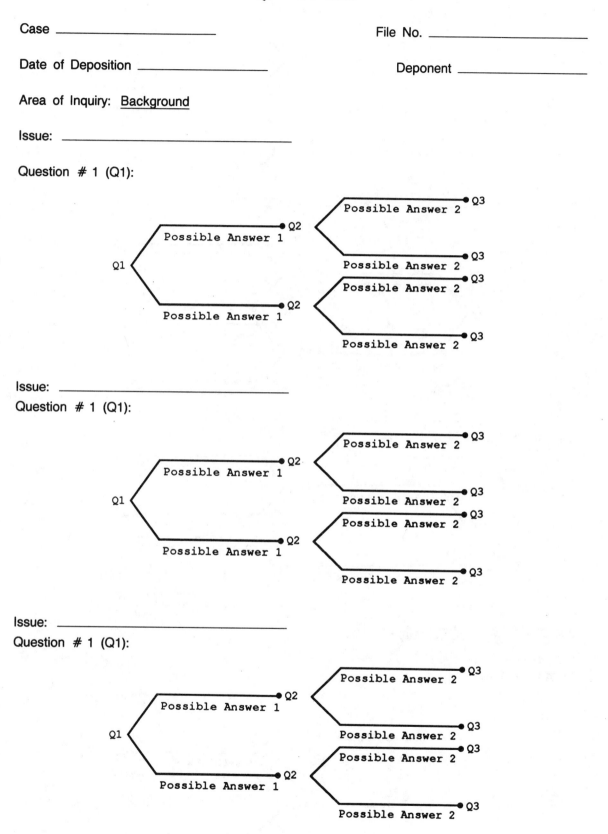

Issue: _____
Question # 1 (Q1):

Issue: _____
Question # 1 (Q1):

Area of Inquiry: <u>Case Facts</u>

Issue: _____

Question # 1 (Q1):

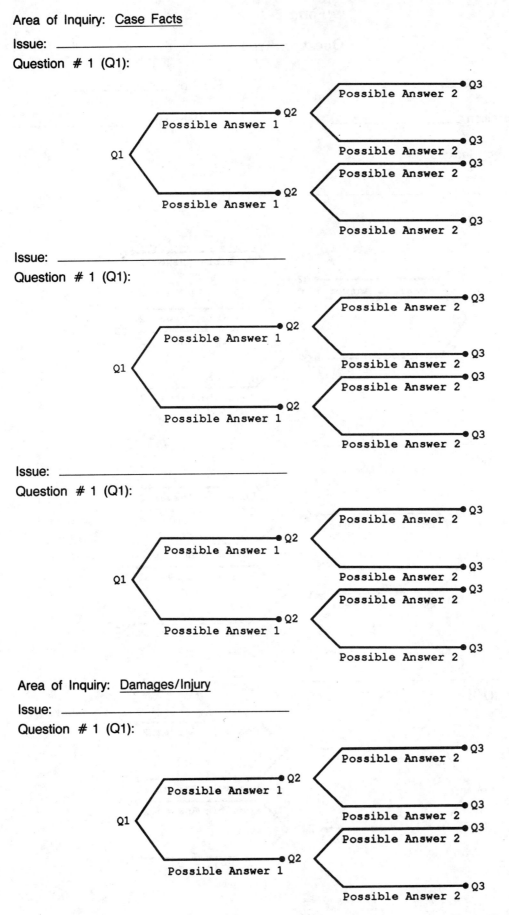

Issue: _____

Question # 1 (Q1):

Issue: _____

Question # 1 (Q1):

Area of Inquiry: <u>Damages/Injury</u>

Issue: _____

Question # 1 (Q1):

Issue: _____

Question # 1 (Q1):

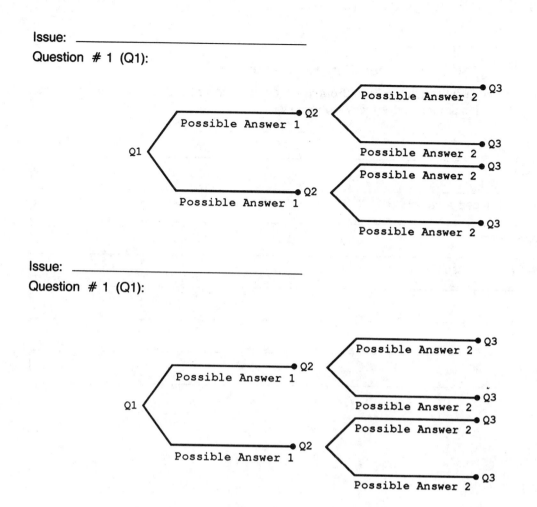

Issue: _____

Question # 1 (Q1):

Form 5–2

Question Evaluation

After completing the Question Outline Tree (Form 5–1), check to insure that all questions meet the following guidelines for proper and effective questions:

Is each question:	Yes	No
relevant?		
avoiding privileged areas?		
in proper form?		
focused on one issue?		
clear?		
brief?		
simple in design?		

Form 5–3

Answer Checklist

Consider each response of the deponent to insure that it is:

Responsive to the question asked:	Y	N
Focused	Y	N
Complete	Y	N
Specific and not ambiguous	Y	N
Not rambling	Y	N
Does not leave the question unclear	Y	N

When any of the above factors cannot be answered with a "Yes," consider what follow up must be undertaken to achieve a proper answer:

Rephrase the question as follows: _____

_____

_____

Re-ask the question with a qualification or clarification as follows: _____

_____

_____

Follow up the question with another question as follows: _____

_____

_____

Chapter 6

MANAGING CONFLICT IN THE DEPOSITION

Table of Sections

---

§ 6.1 Generally

Not surprisingly, attorneys who present their clients for deposition vent their partisan zeal throughout the deposition by obstructing the flow of questions and answers. The examining attorney must understand that his adversary has every incentive to *create* conflict during the deposition in order to obstruct the harmful evidence-gathering process. In meeting the presenting attorney's obstructionist tactics, the examiner, however, must resist the temptation to make those tactics the focal point of the examination. Rather, the examiner must *manage* the conflict in a calm but firm manner. Managing the conflict means, at a minimum, neutralizing the obstructionist tactics of the adversary with clear and direct responses based on the law which governs the deposition interaction. In addition, an attorney skilled in the deposition interaction will actually use the conflict to his advantage.

Conflict is likely to arise during the deposition in the following situations: (1) the use of objections to questions; (2) terminating the deposition; and (3) sanctions for deposition abuse. These conflict situations pose different legal and tactical considerations for deposing and presenting attorneys.

§ 6.2 Objections—Generally

Two kinds of objections arise during a deposition. The presenting attorney may object to a question and instruct his witness not to answer. Alternatively, and much more routinely, the presenting attorney objects to a question in order to preserve that objection for trial or for strategic reasons, knowing that the answer must be given subject to the objection.

Although only an objection based on privilege will justify an instruction not to answer, presenting attorneys often object on other grounds. In order to handle those objections, the deposing attorney must first understand their underlying purpose. Objections cannot be, and typically are not, used to prevent the deponent from responding to a question. In fact, the federal rules expressly provide that evidence objected to at the deposition is taken subject to the objection. Fed.R.Civ.P. 30. Why, then, do presenting attorneys bother to object? They do so for two reasons: to prevent waiver of the objections at trial and to control damage done to the deponent.

§ 6.3 The Law Permitting Instructions Not to Answer

The examination of the deponent "may" proceed as permitted at the trial under the rules of evidence. Fed.R.Civ.P. 30(a). But the Federal Rules do not preclude the examiner from deposing a witness in a manner not permitted at trial. *See* Wright & Miller, 8 Federal Practice & Procedure, § 2113. The only absolute constraints on the deposition examination are provided by the rules governing the scope of discovery. Under the Federal Rules, which are copied in most states (*see* Appendix A), the deposing attorney may inquire into any matter:

(1) not privileged;

(2) relevant to the subject matter involved in the pending action;

(3) which relates to any claim or defense asserted by any party;

(4) including the existence, description, nature, custody, condition, location of any books, documents, or other tangible things; and

(5) including the identity and location of persons having knowledge of other discoverable matter. *See* Fed.R.Civ.P. 26(b)(1).

§ 6.4 Scope Not Proper Ground for Instruction Not to Answer

The Rules expressly state that the presenting attorney may not successfully object to the relevance of the questions so long as the information sought appears reasonably calculated to lead to the discovery of admissible evidence. Fed.R.Civ.P. 26(b)(1). Moreover, the Federal Rules expressly provide that objections made at the time of the deposition, including those directed toward the manner of questioning, the evidence presented or the conduct of the attorneys, shall be noted by the officer, but may not preclude a response. Instead, evidence objected to during the deposition shall be taken at the deposition, subject to the objections which will be ruled upon if they are raised subsequently at trial. Fed.R.Civ.P. 30(c).

The Federal Rules do permit any attorney to seek a protective order in advance of the deposition limiting the scope or manner of questioning. Fed.R.Civ.P. 26(c). They also allow the presenting attorney to terminate the deposition and seek such a protective order. Fed.R. Civ.P. 30(d). In the absence of such a judicial order, however, the Federal Rules do not permit a presenting attorney to instruct his witness not to answer any questions.

§ 6.5 Privilege the Only Proper Ground for Instruction Not to Answer

The courts have relaxed this strict rule, allowing an instruction not to answer a deposition question without a court order in one circumstance: where the question seeks privileged matter. *See e.g.* Perrignon v. Bergen Brunswig Corp., 77 F.R.D. 455 (N.D.Cal.1978). Therefore, the only occasion in which a presenting attorney may legitimately instruct his witness not to respond to a deposition question is when that attorney claims a privilege.

§ 6.6 Privileges—Generally

Three different categories of privilege exist: (1) the attorney-client privilege; (2) the work-product privilege; and (3) additional common law privileges.

§ 6.7 Law Governing Privilege

In determining the propriety of any claim of privilege, the attorneys must understand the source of the privilege and the law which governs its scope. In federal court actions, Federal Rule of Evidence 501 governs the choice of law:

Except as otherwise required by the Constitution of the United States or provided by Act of Congress or in rules prescribed by the Supreme Court pursuant to statutory authority, the privilege of a witness, person, government, state or political subdivision thereof shall be governed by the Courts of the United States in light of reason and experience. However, in civil actions and proceedings, with respect to an element of a claim or defense as to which state law supplies the rule of decision, the privilege of a witness, person, government, state, or political subdivision thereof shall be determined in accordance with state law.

Thus, in pure federal question cases, federal common law governs the scope of privileges. In diversity cases, on the other hand, state common law privileges are applicable. Where both federal and state law claims are pending in the same federal court action, either because diverse claims are joined with federal question claims or because state law claims are pendent to federal question claims, the federal common law of privileges governs both the federal and the state law claims. Finally, in actions brought in state court, the state's common law of privilege governs the action.

§ 6.8 The Attorney–Client Privilege—Generally

The attorney-client privilege, the oldest of privileges known to the common law, is rooted in the belief that if communications between attorneys and clients were discoverable, the client would be reluctant to reveal damaging information to the attorney, and the attorney would be reluctant to counsel the client to alter unlawful conduct. The freezing of information from client to attorney would hamper the attorney's effort to prepare a case or to provide useful advice, while the freezing of information from attorney to client would hamper the attorney's effort to counsel clients in how to obey the law.

The privilege thus has two purposes: (1) it allows attorneys to gather sufficient truthful information in preparation for trial or for counseling and (2) it allows attorneys to use that information to advise clients fully in law-abiding behavior.

§ 6.9 Attorney–Client Privilege—Elements

The purposes of the privilege define its scope. By definition, the claim of privilege requires a showing of the following elements: client, attorney and communication.

First, the person seeking the privilege must be either a client, or someone seeking to become a client, of the attorney with whom the communication was held. Where the client is an individual, this element of the privilege is usually readily satisfied. Where, however, the client is a corporation, a choice of law problem arises. Under federal common law, which governs all federal actions where jurisdiction is not based on diversity alone, the corporate client includes *all* employees within the corporation—not just those in control of its decision-making process—provided that

(1) the employees made the communications to secure legal advice;

(2) the employees made the communications at the direction of their corporate superiors;

(3) the communications concerned matters within the scope of the employees' employment; and

(4) the employees were made aware that they were being questioned so that the corporation could secure legal advice.

See Upjohn Co. v. United States, 449 U.S. 383, 101 S.Ct. 677, 66 L.Ed.2d 584 (1981).

In *Upjohn,* the Supreme Court rejected the "control-group" theory of the attorney-client privilege in the corporate setting. Under that rejected theory, which is still the law in a majority of states, only communications between an attorney and those individuals within the corporate client who are capable of controlling the future decisions of the corporation are shielded by the attorney-client privilege. This control-group privilege is based on the theory that the attorney-client privilege should protect only advisory communications running from the attorney to the corporation. Because only those in "control" of the corporation have the power to act on an attorney's advice, no need exists to protect communications between an attorney and lower level employees.

In rejecting this view for federal actions not based solely on diversity, the Supreme Court found that the purpose of the attorney-client privilege is not only to protect advisory communications from an attorney to those in control of a corporation, it is also to protect the flow of information from a corporate client to the attorney. Because accurate information relevant to pending or potential litigation often emanates from the lowest level employees, communications from such employees to their attorneys should be shielded as well.

While the Supreme Court as a matter of federal common law rejected the control-group definition of a corporate client, that and alternative state law definitions of the corporate client still control state court actions and pure diversity actions in federal court. Before taking the deposition of a corporate client, the attorney must determine whether the federal or state law of privileges will control, and then determine whether the deponent is a "client" under the governing standards. (*See* Appendix B).

Second, the claim of privilege must pertain to a communication to or from an *attorney.* The attorney must be a member of a bar or the subordinate of a member of a bar who is receiving information or giving advice within the scope of his duties as a professional legal adviser. *See e.g.* 8 Wigmore, Evidence, § 2291, at 554 (1961).

Finally, the claim of privilege must, of course, relate to a communication. The communication may be oral or written. But the communication must be made in confidence for the purpose of gaining or giving legal advice.

§ 6.10   Waiver of Attorney–Client Privilege

Even if each of these elements of the attorney-client privilege is present, however, the deposing attorney still has the right to obtain discovery of the privileged material if the privilege has been waived. Waiver can occur either by the client or by the attorney acting on the client's behalf. The attorney-client privilege belongs to the client. Typically, when the client waives the privilege, however, he does so inadvertently at the time the communication is made. The presence of individuals not within the scope of the attorney-client privilege at the time the otherwise privileged communication is given will waive the privilege. Further, the attorney-client privilege does not preclude the discovery of information revealed both to an attorney and independently to someone outside the scope of the privilege.

Although a client may involuntarily waive the privilege, an attorney acting on behalf of the client can do so only by voluntarily consenting to the disclosure. An attorney voluntarily consents to the disclosure of privileged matter when he fails to take reasonable and available steps to prevent disclosure. *See e.g.* Perrignon v. Bergen Brunswig Corp., 77 F.R.D. 455 at 460 (N.D.Cal.1978). Thus, the burden is placed upon the defending attorney to take affirmative steps to prevent disclosure of the privileged communication.

§ 6.11 Preserving the Privilege

The defending attorney has available three reasonable steps to prevent disclosure at deposition of privileged matter. He may anticipate the questioning which approaches privileged matter and seek a protective order before the deposition. Fed.R.Civ.P. 26(c). Alternatively, the defending attorney may terminate the deposition when questions arise regarding the privileged matter and then seek a protective order. Fed.R.Civ.P. 30(d). Finally, for the sole purpose of avoiding the waiver of an available attorney-client privilege, the attorney may instruct the witness not to answer.

§ 6.12 The Work–Product Doctrine—Generally

Under the work-product doctrine, which is not technically a privilege, the federal courts permit discovery of tangible materials prepared in anticipation of trial by a party or its agent, only if the discovering party can show a substantial need for the materials and that the materials cannot without undue hardship be obtained by alternative means. *See* Fed.R.Civ.P. 26(b)(3). Moreover, the Federal Rules mandate that even if the federal court permits discovery upon this affirmative showing, it must enter a protective order precluding discovery of the mental impressions, conclusions, opinions, or legal theories of the party's attorney or other agent concerning the litigation.

§ 6.13 Burden to Obtain Discovery

Although the Federal Rules preclude the discovery of such mental impressions, the Supreme Court in Upjohn Co. v. United States, 449 U.S. 383, 101 S.Ct. 677, 66 L.Ed.2d 584 (1981), suggested a sliding scale of protection: the closer the information is to intangible mental impressions, the greater the showing of substantial need and undue hardship that is required. In any event, the discovering party can, without any showing at all, discover statements made *by that party* whether or not such a statement will be used by the adversary in preparation for litigation. Fed.R.Civ.P. 26(b)(3).

Unlike the attorney-client privilege, which places the burden on the presenting party to object to deposition questions to avoid a waiver of the privilege, the work-product doctrine places the burden on the deposing party to make an affirmative showing that the desired information should be discovered. Hence, if the deposing attorney anticipates that work-product will be sought during the deposition, he should, in accord with the Federal Rules, seek an order allowing such discovery in advance of the deposition.

§ 6.14 Handling Objections to Work–Product Protection

If the pursuit of work-product material cannot be anticipated or if the deposing attorney does not wish to tip his hand before the deposition, he should be prepared for a proper objection to his questioning regarding such material. In that situation, he should force the defending attorney to state his objection and its grounds. He should voice his disagreement with the objection for the record and do one of the following: (a) terminate the deposition if the challenged questioning is a significant portion of the entire deposition and seek a court order allowing the discovery, (b) phone a judge or magistrate in the district where the deposition is being taken and seek such an order over the phone, or (c) continue with the deposition, stating for the record that the deposition is not completed and will be re-opened after such time as the court may rule on the requested discovery.

In attempting to make the showing necessary to obtain work-product material, the deposing attorney may argue that the material sought (1) was not prepared in anticipation of litigation or trial, (2) was not prepared by an attorney or other agent of a party, (3) includes statements made by the deposing party, (4) is crucial to the case and cannot be obtained by other means or (5) has been disclosed to third-parties who are not agents of the party for purposes of litigation, and thus, the privilege has been waived.

§ 6.15 Additional Common Law Privileges

In federal actions based solely on diversity and in state court actions, the applicable state common law privileges supply additional grounds for the instruction not to answer a deposition question. Although each state has developed its own evidentiary privileges, most protect communications between:

(1) husband and wife;

(2) physician and patient;

(3) clergy and penitent;

(4) journalist and source;

(5) governmental officials.

Some states, in addition, recognize a privilege between accountant and client, and teacher and pupil. *See* 8 Wigmore, Evidence § 2286 (1961).

§ 6.16 Responding to an Instruction Not to Answer

If the defending attorney instructs his witness not to answer a deposition question, the deposing attorney should pursue the following course:

First, calmly ensure that the witness has in fact been instructed not to answer.

Second, if the witness has effectively been instructed not to answer, request the defending attorney to state for the record that such instruction has been given. A clear instruction not to answer on the record will be useful should any judicial action be required.

Third, inquire into the scope of the instruction not to answer.

Fourth, if the defending attorney insists on maintaining a blanket instruction not to answer, consult the law governing the proper use of instructions not to answer. Unless the instruction not to answer is based on a claim of privilege, it is patently improper. If the instruction is based on the attorney-client or other common law privilege, it is not well-taken if the privilege does not apply or if it has been waived. Finally, if the instruction not to answer is based on the work-product doctrine, the deposing attorney should anticipate securing a court order before proceeding with the challenged area of inquiry.

Fifth, if the instruction not to answer is proper, offer to accommodate the objection by inquiring into alternative areas, or by approaching the same area in another way. Even if the instruction not to answer is improper, maintain a conciliatory tone. A calm but firm statement, reminding the defending attorney and the *witness* that the attorney's improper conduct is prolonging the deposition and may force the witness to return on another day, can do more to compel a response than a race to the courthouse.

Finally, if the presenting attorney persists in his improper obstruction of a proper question, the deposing attorney should then consider seeking judicial relief.

§ 6.17 Objections to Prevent Waiver

If the grounds for an objection can be removed at the time of the deposition, the presenting party waives the objection by failing to make it at that time. Fed.R.Civ.P. 32(3)(A)(B). If, on the other hand, the basis for the objection cannot be removed at the taking of the deposition, the presenting party cannot waive the objection by failing to raise it at deposition. The purpose of this waiver rule is to force the presenting attorney to object at a point in the litigation when the alleged error in the deposition can be cured. If the presenting party is permitted to wait until trial to raise an objection, the objection cannot be cured and the trial judge is forced to exclude entirely the objectionable portions from the trial. The rule is intended to discourage presenting attorneys from waiting until trial before making any objections in the hope that the testimony will be excluded altogether because of the manner in which it was elicited. *See e.g.* Bahamas Agr. Industries Ltd. v. Riley Stoker Corp., 526 F.2d 1174, 1181 (6th Cir.1975).

Despite the rule, presenting attorneys often decide *not* to raise an obvious objection during the deposition so as not to instruct the deposing attorney in how the objectionable questioning may be cured. The presenting attorney often complements this strategy by getting a stipulation from the deposing attorney that all objections except those "as to form" are reserved.

In responding to this approach, the deposing attorney should first reject any such stipulation. The familiar refrain that "objections except as to form are preserved" does not accurately reflect the rule. The rule requires the presenting attorney to object at deposition to all matters which "might" at that time be cured. *See* Fed.R.Civ.P. 32(d)(3)(A). Hence, the deposing attorney should simply state for the record that the Federal Rules governing the deposition procedure shall apply, thereby forcing the presenting attorney to make proper objections at the time of the deposition.

But the deposing attorney cannot count on the trial court's strict enforcement of the waiver rule. Objections are rarely waived, even if they are based on defects which might have been cured. Thus, the safest course for the deposing attorney to follow is to ask questions which are not objectionable. Questions which are objectionable because they are compound, argumentative, cumulative, vague, hypothetical, based on facts which are incorrect or not established or call for information the witness is not competent to provide are bad deposition questions.

§ 6.18 Asking "Bad" Questions—An Advantage

On the other hand, such questions can, despite their formal flaws, be useful tools in discovering facts. If the examining attorney's primary goal in asking a question is to discover facts which may lead to the discovery of additional evidence which is admissible at trial, then the question's improper form may actually foster that goal. A vague question, for example, can induce the witness to provide testimony not even contemplated by the examiner. Similarly, a hypothetical question can induce the witness to volunteer damaging information. Asking a question which the witness is incompetent to answer may induce that witness (or his lawyer) to suggest or state his lack of knowledge of an entire subject area. The examining attorney, however, must be aware that apart from their value in discovery, objectionable questions do not provide a clean evidentiary record for trial. Thus, by understanding the purposes of an objection, the examining attorney can either avoid the objection by framing a non-objectionable question or can use the objection to his advantage.

§ 6.19 Objections to Control Damage

Most objections at a deposition are neither intended to protect privileged material nor to cure an objectionable question. Rather, the objection is used by the presenting attorney as a device for limiting the damage which may be done to the deponent.

§ 6.20 Response to Coaching the Deponent—Generally

If the examining attorney recognizes the objection to be merely a method of coaching the witness, he should consider the following alternative responses: no response, restating the question verbatim, re-phrase the question, meet the objection, seek judicial relief.

§ 6.21 No Response to Objection

Unless the presenting attorney has expressly instructed the deponent not to respond, the question must be answered despite the objection. The examining attorney should inform the deponent of this rule, preferably once at the start of the deposition. Then, when an objection is raised, the examiner may obtain a response to a pending question simply by making prolonged eye contact with the witness or by nodding the head as if to indicate that the witness should proceed.

The lack of any verbal response to an objection has several advantages. It minimizes the objection, minimizes the conflict, isolates the objecting attorney from the examination and results in a transcript in which the deposition answer is not separated from the deposition question by pages of speeches regarding the objection.

The lack of any response to the objection, however, can create the impression of passivity or tolerance to frequent subsequent objections. It also has the disadvantage of leaving the transcript less clear than it could be: the deposition question will be separated from the deposition answer by a lawyer's objection to the question. Finally, the absence of any response, of course, cannot cure questions which truly are improper in form.

§ 6.22 Response to Objection—Restate the Question Verbatim

Responding to an objection by merely restating the question verbatim has many of the advantages of no response at all. This method of managing conflict not only minimizes the objection, it helps re-assert the examiner's control over the interaction. Moreover, it has the added advantage of leaving a clean transcript: the answer presumably follows immediately from the restated question.

Merely restating the original question, however, does have the disadvantage of inviting a restatement of the objection. It also may result in the repetition of a question which is improper as to form.

§ 6.23 Response to Objection—Re-phrase the Question

Ideally, all objections as to the form of a deposition question would be well-taken and would result in a re-phrasing of the question so as to make it proper. If the objection is well-taken (*i.e.* the question was vague or compound), the examiner should, without discussion, re-phrase it—maintaining eye contact with the witness. Even if the objection is not well-taken, however, the examiner should consider re-phrasing the next question to cure the alleged defect and returning to the original question later in the deposition.

This approach has the advantage of minimizing the conflict which objections can create. Often, the examining attorney will be able to return to the original question at a later time in the deposition without receiving the previous objection. Alternatively, the deposition testimony may render the original question unnecessary.

Re-phrasing a question in response to an objection, however, does have disadvantages. The act of re-phrasing is somewhat of a concession to the adversary. It displays an insecurity in the propriety of the original question. And it allows the presenting attorney to control the form and timing of the deposition questions.

§ 6.24 Response to Objection—Meet the Objection

Lawyers cannot resist a good argument. So when an objection comes at a deposition, the examiner's instinctual response is to fight the objection; confrontation should be a last resort. One lawyer's argument merely breeds another lawyer's response. The result at a deposition is that a relatively innocuous objection can become the focal point of the entire deposition, consuming precious energy, time and transcript pages. Hence, the examiner should resist the temptation to engage the presenter in a speechmaking contest.

Nonetheless, there are situations in which the examiner should make some statement about the objection itself. First, if the objection is patently wrong and such can be demonstrated by the examiner, a response may be appropriate.

Second, if the defending attorney repeatedly objects, a warning may be appropriate. The first warnings should be directed not to the attorney, but to the witness. Statements such as the following are useful: "Mr. Witness, it is now 3:00 o'clock. I had hoped to be able to complete this deposition today. But your attorney insists on interrupting you before you can answer my questions. He understands that despite his objections, you must answer my questions. Still, he insists on prolonging this deposition and is wasting your time."

Third, the examiner may respond to an objection by asking *the witness* whether he felt the question was unanswerable. The following exchange illustrates this method:

Q. When did you first read the Prospectus?

Defending Attorney: Objection. The question is vague—which prospectus? during what time frame?

Deposing Attorney: (To the witness) Were you incapable of understanding my question? You understood which prospectus I was referring to, didn't you?

A. Yes. I first read the prospectus this morning in preparation for my deposition.

Fourth, the deposing attorney can respond to the objection by using it to confuse the witness, or lead him in different directions. A similar interaction illustrates this approach:

Q. When did you first read the Prospectus?

Defending Attorney: Objection. The question assumes facts not in evidence.

Deposing Attorney: Your objection is well-taken. My question improperly assumes that the witness read the prospectus. I will re-phrase it.

Q. You never read the prospectus, did you?

A. No.

Forms 6–1 thru 6–5 help the examining attorney to manage conflict within the deposition without resorting to judicial relief.

§ 6.25   Response to Objection—Seek Judicial Relief

The deposing attorney confronted with obstructionist objections may also seek a court order compelling deposition answers, Fed.R.Civ.P. 37(a). The deposing attorney may complete or adjourn the deposition before seeking such an order.

§ 6.26   Compelling Deposition Responses

Ultimately, the deposing attorney may handle the adversary's obstructionist tactics by seeking judicial relief. The Federal Rules, followed in most states (*See* Appendix A), provide a procedure which the frustrated examiner must follow in order to get that relief.

§ 6.27   Procedure to Compel Deposition Response

First, the rules permit the examiner to decide *when* to seek an order compelling testimony. Fed.R.Civ.P. 37(a)(2). The order may be obtained either after the deposition has been completed or by adjourning the deposition. Adjourning the deposition can be done formally or informally. The deposing attorney may state for the record that the deposition cannot, because of the adversary's obstructionist tactics, be completed and that it will be adjourned until such time as a court order is obtained. Alternatively, the deposing attorney can state for the record that the deposition will be adjourned until such time as a court order can be obtained by telephone. Although the Federal Rules do not expressly authorize the issuance of a court order compelling deposition testimony by telephone, they do allow motions for such orders and do authorize the federal courts to manage the entire discovery process by entering appropriate orders, Fed.R.Civ.P. 26(b)(c)(3)(f). Furthermore, local rule and custom frequently dictate that truly unresolveable deposition conflicts be submitted to the judge by telephone.

While adjournment to obtain a court order before completing a deposition is possible, it should be used only where the adversary makes it impossible to continue. Rather, the best procedure is to complete the deposition in areas not subject to controversy, and then seek an order compelling testimony. In doing so, however, the deposing attorney should be careful to state for the record that the deposition has not been completed and will be continued after the court rules on motions to compel.

Second, whether by telephone or in person, the examiner must actually seek a court order compelling the deposition witness to answer questions.

Third, the deposing party must ensure that all parties and persons affected by the motion receive reasonable notice of that motion. Presumably, this notice provision requires "conferencing" into a telephonic motion to compel all affected persons.

Fourth, the deposing attorney must decide whether to file the motion in the district court where the deposition is being taken or where the action is pending. The motion to compel a party's deposition responses can be filed in, or the telephone call made to, either the district court in which the action is pending or in which the deposition is being taken. Fed.R.Civ.P. 37(a)(1). If, however, the deponent is a non-party, the motion must be made to the district court in which the deposition is being taken. Fed.R.Civ.P. 37(a)(1).

§ 6.28 Motion to Compel—Court Power

Both the court where the deposition is being taken and the court where the action is pending have the power to award fees and expenses relative to the motion to compel. But the sanctions available differ for the court in which the action is pending and where the deposition occurs. The court where the deposition is being taken has no authority to affect the underlying litigation. Instead, it may sanction a failure to comply with its compulsion order only by finding the deponent or his attorney in contempt. On the other hand, the court where the action is pending has no power to sanction non-parties for their failure to follow a court order issued by the district court where the deposition is being taken.

But the district court where the action is pending does have a battery of sanctions for a party's failure to comply with a court order issued either by that court or by the court in which the deposition is being taken. The sanctions for a party's failure to comply with a court order include:

(1) Entry of an order that matters related to the deposition are deemed established;

(2) Entry of an order refusing to allow the deponent to support or oppose designated claims or defenses;

(3) Entry of an order precluding the adversary from introducing designated matters into evidence;

(4) Entry of an order striking the party's claims, defenses or parts thereof;

(5) Entry of an order of dismissal or default; and

(6) Expenses and fees incurred as a result of the non-compliance. Fed.R.Civ.P. 37(b).

§ 6.29 Motion to Compel—Sanctions

The deposing party may seek two kinds of sanctions for an adversary's failure to answer deposition questions: an award of the expenses for the motion itself, and sanctions for failure to comply with any resulting order.

As a general rule, the party who loses a motion to compel deposition responses must pay the victor's expenses relative to the motion. The court in which the motion to compel is filed must require the adversary (the deponent or his attorney) to pay the moving party the reasonable expenses and fees in obtaining the court order, unless the court finds that the adversary's opposition to the motion was justified or that sanctions would otherwise be unjust. If on the other hand the court denies the motion to compel, it must award the non-moving party the expenses and fees incurred in responding to the motion, unless the court finds that the motion was justified or that such an award would be otherwise unjust. Finally, the court may apportion expenses if it decides to grant the motion only in part. Fed.R.Civ.P. 37(a)(4).

The rule creates a presumption in favor of awarding sanctions against the party who loses the motion to compel. The presumption can be rebutted only if the losing party affirmatively shows that his position was "substantially justified." A losing position is not substantially justified merely because the loser in good faith believed his position to be valid. Instead, courts, in keeping with the standards for imposing sanctions under Federal Rule of Civil Procedure 11, follow an objective test. Where a "reasonable" attorney in the jurisdiction would consider the loser's position to be justified, no sanctions will be awarded. *See* Wright & Miller, 8 Federal Practice & Procedure, § 2288.

Sanctions are also available where the deponent or his attorney fails to comply with a court order compelling deposition responses. If the district court in which the deposition is being taken issues an order to respond to deposition questions which is disobeyed, that court may find the deponent or his attorney in contempt of court. Fed.R.Civ.P. 37(b)(1). If a party fails to obey an order entered either by the court where the action is pending or where the deposition is being taken, the court where the action is pending may enter the additional Fed. R.Civ.P. 37(b)(2) sanctions.

§ 6.30 Motion to Compel—Court Discretion

In ruling on the motion to compel deposition responses, the district court has wide discretion. If the defending attorney's objections are generally proper, the motion will be denied. *See e.g.* In re Folding Carton Antitrust Litigation, 83 F.R.D. 132 (N.D.Ill.1979). If, at the other end of the spectrum, the defending attorney improperly instructed his witness not to answer numerous questions, the district court will order the questions answered on penalty of default for failure to do so. *See e.g.* Penn Communications Specialities, Inc. v. Hess, 65 F.R.D. 510 (E.D.Pa.1975).

§ 6.31 Motion to Compel—Factors

For conduct which falls within these two extremes, however, the district court's decision to compel testimony will be guided by the totality of the circumstances, including (1) the importance of the witness to the litigation; (2) the burden on the witness; (3) the importance of the questions relative to the deposition; (4) the length of the deposition thus far; (5) the possibility of obtaining the same information by other means; and (6) the gravity of the obstructionist tactics. *See* Wright & Miller, 8 Federal Practice & Procedure, § 2286. Form 6–7 catalogues the various forms of judicial relief available to the deposing attorney.

Deposition Objections and Instructions Not to Answer

Objection	Purpose	Instructions Not to Answer Proper
1. Privilege	Prevent waiver of privilege.	Yes.
2. Scope	Prevent damage control by intimidation or coaching.	No; *see e.g.,* Eggleston v. Chicago Journeyman, 657 F.2d 890 (7th Cir.1981), cert. denied, 455 U.S. 1017 (1982).
3. Form—Vague, compound, competentcy	Prevent waiver of objection, the grounds for which could have been removed at the time of deposition.	No; *see* Fed.R.Civ.P. 30(c).
4. Speaking	To coach the witness.	No; *see* Fed.R.Civ.P. 30(c).

Form 6–2

Deposition Objections Generally

Questions	Objections	Basis	Response	Follow-up

Form 6–3

Propriety of Instructions Not to Answer—
The Attorney–Client Privilege

Elements of Privilege	Authority	Elements Present?

1. Attorney
  (a) Member of bar, or
  (b) Subordinate of member of bar
  (c) Acting in professional capacity
	Upjohn; Wigmore	

2. Client
  (a) Seeker of legal advice, or
  (b) Seeking to be a client
  (c) If corporation:
    (1) Federal actions not based solely on diversity
    (a) any employee
    (b) giving information within scope of employment
    (2) Other actions—
    (a) state law?
    (b) control group?
	Id.	

3. Communication
  (a) For purpose of seeking or giving legal advice
  (b) Confidential
	Id.	

4. Waiver?
  (a) By client inadvertently
  (b) By attorney voluntarily		

Form 6-4

The Propriety of Instruction Not to Answer—The Work–Product Doctrine

Elements of Doctrine	Elements Present	Notes
(1) Documents and tangible things other than statement previously made by deposing party.		
(2) Prepared in anticipation of litigation or trial.		
(3) By attorney or agent of party.		

Elements of Showing	Showing Made	Notes
(1) Substantial need.		
(2) Undue hardship to obtain material by other means.		
(3) Extraordinary need if materials are mental impressions of an attorney or agent of party.		

Form 6–5

Objection Responses

Objection	Alternative Responses	Response Chosen
(1) Privilege	(1) Accommodate objection by leaving area or approaching another way	
(2) Scope	(1) No response (2) Restate question verbatim (3) Rephrase question (4) Meet objection (5) Seek court relief	
(3) Form	(1) No response (2) Restate question verbatim (3) Re-phrase question (4) Meet objection (5) Seek court relief	
(4) Coaching	(1) No response (2) Restate question verbatim (3) Rephrase question (4) Meet objection (5) Seek court relief	

Form 6–6

Deposing Attorney's Judicial Relief

Party Deponent	Non-party Deponent

(1) Motion to compel deposition cooperation made either in:
 	
  (a) District court where deposition is action pending (preferable given sanctions) or
 	
  (b) District court where deposition is being taken.
	(1) Motion to compel deposition cooperation made in district court where deposition is being taken.

(2) Motion made either:
 	
  (a) upon completion of deposition, or
 	
  (b) upon adjournment.
	(2) Motion made either:
	
	  (a) upon completion of deposition, or
	
	  (b) upon adjournment.

(3) Motion reasonably noticed to:
 	
  (a) all parties, and
 	
  (b) all persons affected by the motion.
	(3) Motion reasonably noticed to:
	
	  (a) all parties, and
	
	  (b) all persons affected by the motion.

(4) Motion made either:
 	
  (a) formally in writing or
 	
  (b) by telephone at deposition.
	(4) Motion made either:
	
	  (a) formally in writing or
	
	  (b) by telephone at deposition.

(5) Seek award of fees and expenses upon motion, if successful.	(5) Seek award of fees and expenses upon motion, if successful.

(6) Seek sanction for failure to comply with order:
 	
  (a) finding of contempt if order entered by court where deposition is being taken, and
 	
  (b) Rule 37(b)(2) Sanctions.
	(6) Seek contempt sanction for failure to comply with order.

Chapter 7

DEPOSING ATTORNEY'S POST–DEPOSITION PROCEDURES

Table of Sections

---

§ 7.1 Generally

The deposition does not end when the final question is answered. Rather, the deposition testimony must be transcribed, submitted to the witness, signed, certified by the officer, and in some cases filed with an appropriate court. Seemingly routine, these procedures can create changes in testimony and problems at trial which will undo an otherwise successful deposition. Accordingly, attorneys must understand these post-deposition procedures and ensure that they are not being used by the adversary in a way which jeopardizes the deposition testimony.

§ 7.2 Preparing a Deposition Summary

As soon as possible after the deposition concludes, the examining attorney should dictate or draft a summary memorandum to the file of the deposition proceedings. Whether or not the transcript of the deposition was ordered written, a summary memorandum written in narrative form provides the attorney with an essential tool of review and preparation for subsequent depositions and trial. Form 7–1 provides a format for summarizing the deposition, while Form 7–2 provides a post-deposition checklist.

§ 7.3 Deposition Summary Format

The summary should begin with the names of all present, including the court reporter, the court reporting service and whether the transcript was ordered written. This will help clear what later will be forgotten. Next, a detailed narrative of all information gathered at the deposition follows. The summary need not be written in the order the information was gathered, since the examiner likely shifted around in follow-up and probing. The summary should be a coherent and complete picture of the testimony. The final section of the summary is a detailed statement of witness and attorney demeanor as well as specific comments on the manner in which the deponent responded to questions and the type of witness that the deponent will likely make at trial.

It should be clear that this summary document is an essential part of case development as it reflects not only substantive information, but the examining attorney's work product and thought. These summaries are often referenced for planning settlement or trial.

§ 7.4 Client Letter

A separate document, often in the form of a letter to the client, should be prepared which summarizes the important aspects of the deposition. This letter or memorandum pulls together by case issue, legal argument, or defense the crucial information uncovered at the deposition and how that information impacts the present and future status of the litigation. This brief summary letter (often no more than a page and a half long) evaluates case posture. The summary letter and the complete deposition summary are both forwarded to the client for review and consideration. A summary transcript should be prepared in all cases, whether or not a transcript is ordered written; questions may arise before the transcript is completed or other depositions may occur before the transcript is received. Integrating lawyer impressions and thoughts into the memorandum qualifies the summary as work product and may entitle it to an absolute privilege in accordance with Fed.R.Civ.P. 26(b)(3). The summary letter also provides an economical means of keeping track of the deposition without undertaking the cost of transcription early in the litigation.

§ 7.5 The Accurate Transcript

Where the transcript as prepared is accurate and there is no reason to request any relief concerning the transcript from the reporter or the court, the examiner must decide whether or not to file the transcript. While Fed.R.Civ.P. 30(f)(1) apparently requires filing, many jurisdictions do not have the attorneys file the deposition transcripts unless they are going to be used at trial. Where the transcript will be part of a motion for summary judgment to be filed in the case, the transcript should be filed. If the transcript is going to be relied upon at a motion hearing and has not been filed, the attorney may not simply rely on the contents of the transcript but must prepare a special appendix for its submission on motion. Blumenkopf, Deposition Strategy and Tactics. If the transcript is filed, the filing deadlines in each jurisdiction must be followed.

§ 7.6 Errors in the Transcript

Where a transcript contains mistakes or requires modification, or the deponent or other attorney abused the opportunity to correct the transcript as a pretext for adding favorable facts, there are several options available to the attorney: (1) motion for a re-deposition; (2) motion to compel further answers to particular questions; (3) motion to strike particular portions of the transcript; (4) motion to suppress the transcript; or (5) motion to suppress testimony by the deponent.

§ 7.7 Submission of Record to the Witness

After the deposition is fully transcribed, or recorded in some readily discernible fashion, the record must be

    (1) submitted to the witness;

    (2) examined by the witness;

    (3) read to or by the witness; and

    (4) ultimately signed by the witness. Fed.R.Civ.P. 30(e).

The purpose for allowing the witness to examine the record is so that he can make any changes on that record before signature. The rules permit changes in form or substance, provided that the witness provides reasons for making them. Fed.R.Civ.P. 30(e). While it may be improper or imprudent for witnesses to make radical substantive changes in a deposition record, they often do so to erase damaging testimony. The examiner, therefore, should try to prevent such changes whenever possible.

§ 7.8 Obtaining Waiver of Deponent's Rights

The easiest way to prevent the deponent from altering damaging deposition testimony is to get the deponent to waive his right to read and sign the record. The rules provide that examination, reading and signature can all be waived by the parties and the witness. Fed.R. Civ.P. 30(e).

Waiver can be involuntary. If the witness, for whatever reason, does not sign the deposition within 30 days of its submission to him, he will be deemed to have waived signature. In that instance, the officer signs the deposition and it can be used as if it were signed by the witness, unless, on a motion to suppress under Fed.R.Civ.P. 32(d)(4), the court finds that the stated reasons for failure to sign justify its suppression.

More often, the deponent and his attorney voluntarily waive signature. In fact, it is common practice for them to do so at the close of the deposition. *See e.g.,* Erstad v. Curtis Bay Towing Co., 28 F.R.D. 583, 584 (D.Md.1961). The mere physical presence of opposing counsel without an affirmative statement of waiver is not enough to constitute such a waiver. Bernstein v. Brenner, 51 F.R.D. 9 (D.C.D.C.1970). Instead, the examiner should secure from opposing counsel an indication of waiver of signature on the record.

Typically, the question whether the deponent waives signature comes from the court reporter. As such, the question takes on less significance than it would if it comes from counsel. From the examiner's point of view, it is beneficial to create the impression that "signature" is a routine mechanical requirement that is "always" waived. Allowing the court reporter to ask the question may reinforce that impression.

Alternatively, the examiner may want to preempt the question by concealing it within a broader question to the court reporter about post-deposition procedures. For example: "How fast can you transcribe this testimony and get it to our office in its completed form?"

If the question is put directly to the witness, the examiner may be able to influence a response. The examination has been completed. The witness feels relaxed, and may even let his guard down. At that point, witnesses sometimes feel that they never want to think about their deposition performance again, let alone *read* it. The examiner can take advantage of this atmosphere by suggesting to the witness that few people read the transcript. Whatever approach taken by the examiner, he should attempt to obtain a waiver of signature.

§ 7.9 Challenging Deponent Changes to Transcript

If the witness does not waive signature, the examiner must scrutinize any changes which the witness makes before signature. Forms 7–3 thru 7–7 allow the attorney to catalogue, scrutinize, respond to and ultimately use at trial any changes that have been made.

§ 7.10 Formalities of Modifying the Transcript

The examiner should ensure that the deponent's changes are formally correct. Those changes must be placed on the original deposition record by the officer. They cannot be made by the witness alone. *See* Architectural League of New York v. Bartos, 404 F.Supp. 304, 311 (S.D.N.Y.1975). If the deposition is recorded by other than stenographic means, the changes must nonetheless be made in writing to accompany the record. Fed.R.Civ.P. 30(b)(4). The original deposition answers must remain as part of the record, with the changes accompanying those answers.

In addition, the witness must provide, and the officer must record, reasons for the changes. Fed.R.Civ.P. 30(e). The courts are split on the degree of particularity required in stating reasons for changes in deposition testimony. Some courts will accept a changed transcript without any explanation for the changes. *See, e.g.,* Bongiovanni v. N.v. Stoomvaart–Matts

"Oostzee", 458 F.Supp. 602, 605 (S.D.N.Y.1978). Most courts, however, require a specific reason for each change. This view was persuasively expressed in Lugtig v. Thomas, 89 F.R.D. 639 (N.D.Ill.1981). There, the court found general conclusory reasons given for all the changes at the end [of the deposition] not sufficient; "after each change, the deponent must state the specific reason for that particular change." 89 F.R.D. at 641. *See* also Sanford v. CBS, Inc., 594 F.Supp. 713, 715 (N.D.Ill.1984).

If the changes are not made formally, the examining attorney should move to strike the changes. This motion to strike, however, will likely be denied. Instead, the court will order that the deposition be amended at the deponent's expense so that the original answer, the changed answer and the reasons for the change appear after each question affected by the changes. Lugtig v. Thomas, 89 F.R.D. 639 at 641 (N.D.Ill.1981).

§ 7.11 The Substance of Changes

The Federal Rules allow deponents to make any changes "in form or substance" which they desire. Fed.R.Civ.P. 30(e). Those changes are proper even if they totally contradict the original answers. Allen & Co. v. Occidental Petroleum Corp., 49 F.R.D. 337 (S.D.N.Y.1970). The reasons for the changes need not be convincing. Lugtig v. Thomas, 89 F.R.D. 639 at 641 (N.D.Ill.1981). So long as the proper procedures for making the changes have been followed, the court will not "examine the sufficiency, reasonableness, or legitimacy of the reasons for the changes." Sanford v. CBS, Inc., 594 F.Supp. 713 at 714 (N.D.Ill.1984).

If the number or nature of changes make the deposition incomplete or useless, the examining party may move to reopen the examination. Courts will allow the deposing attorney to ask additional questions made necessary by the changed answers, including questions about the reasons for the changes and whether they were made by the witness or by counsel. Sanford v. CBS, Inc., 594 F.Supp. 713 at 715 (N.D.Ill.1984). The deponent bears the cost and attorneys fees associated with the reconvening. Lugtig v. Thomas, 89 F.R.D. 639 at 642 (N.D.Ill.1981).

§ 7.12 Using the Deponent's Changes at Trial

Even if the examining attorney cannot prevent changes to deposition testimony, he can use them to his advantage at trial. Since the original answer to the deposition question remains part of the deposition record, together with the changes, both the original answers and the changes can be read into evidence at trial. Usiak v. New York Tank Barge Co., 299 F.2d 808 (2d Cir.1962). If, for example, the disparity between the original deposition answer and the changed answer is a gross one, and reasons for the disparity are unpersuasive, the deposing attorney may choose to forego a challenge to the change to use them for their tremendous impeachment value at trial.

§ 7.13 Certification of the Transcript

The examining attorney must ensure that the deposition has been properly certified. The officer before whom the deposition was taken must certify that the witness was properly sworn and that the deposition contains a true record of the testimony. Fed.R.Civ.P. 30(f). The examining party should make sure that any documents produced during the examination or used during questioning are marked for identification and attached to the deposition. The "originals" of such documents need not be attached if the person producing them offers copies of the originals and allows all parties to verify their replication of the originals. Fed.R.Civ.P. 30(f). Alternatively, the documents need not be annexed to the deposition itself if the producing party retains the originals after marking them for identification and after giving the other parties an opportunity to copy and inspect them.

Although annexation of the original documents to the deposition is unnecessary, it is desirable. The deposing attorney may move for an order that the original be annexed to the deposition if the producing party refuses to cooperate. Fed.R.Civ.P. 30(f)(1).

§ 7.14 Filing the Transcript

After the deposition has been properly certified, the officer must file the deposition in the court where the action is pending, unless the court orders otherwise. Fed.R.Civ.P. 30(f). The Federal Rules encourage orders that depositions need not be filed. But absent such an order or in state jurisdictions where depositions must be filed, the deposing attorney must ensure proper filing, usually by the court reporter or other officer. The deposition may be filed directly with the court or sent by registered or certified mail to the clerk. It is the officer's responsibility to file the deposition. But the examining attorney should make sure that the officer has done so.

Moreover, the Rules provide that the deposition must be (1) securely sealed in an envelope, (2) endorsed with the title of the action, and (3) marked, "Deposition of _____." Fed.R.Civ.P. 30(f). Finally, it is the deposing attorney's responsibility to give "prompt" notice to all other parties that the deposition has been filed. Fed.R.Civ.P. 30(f)(3).

§ 7.15 Expedited Transcription

Once the deposition has been properly filed, the officer must for a "reasonable" fee furnish a copy to the deponent and to any party. In cases of expedited discovery or special urgency, the deposing attorney should make sure that the officer transcribes the testimony on an expedited basis. Expedited transcription, however, can be very expensive. Accordingly, if both parties desire copies on an expedited basis, they may agree that only one of them should request it of the court reporter and then make internal copies for the other. The two parties can then split the court-reporting cost for a single expedited transcript. Alternatively, if the deposing attorney has an ongoing relationship with the reporting service or a poor relationship with the adversary, he may want to force the adversary to incur the additional expense of an expedited transcript.

Deposition Summary

Attention Mark	Substantive Notes
to follow up	
to probe	
to clarify	
to reconsider later after other information is gathered	

Form 7–2

Deposing Party's Post–Deposition Checklist

Deponent: _____

_____ Deponent's Signature

_____ Signature Expressly Waived

_____ Signature Waived by Lapse of 30 Days

_____ Signature Waived by Unavailability of Deponent

_____ Changes Made Correctly

_____ Changes Made in Margin Next to Original Answers

_____ Original Answers Retained

_____ Reasons Given for Changes Made

_____ Reasons Provided for Each Change

_____ Reasons Adequate

_____ Changes Challenged

_____ Changes Used at Trial

Form 7-3

Catalogue of Changes

Deponent: _____

Questions	Tr. Pg.	Original Answer	Tr. Pg.	Change	Reason	Notes on Case at Trial

Form 7–4

Deposing Party's Scrutiny of Changes

Deponent: _____

| Original | Change | Tr. Pg. | Procedural Adequacy | | | | Reasons Adequate | Judicial Relief Necessary |
			Signature Reserved	Changes Made in 30 Days	Original Retained	Reasons Given		

Form 7-5

Deposing Party's Response to Changes

Deponent:_____ by _____

1. Motion to strike change, if
   (a) Signature waived, by
       1. Express statement on record at deposition.
       2. Lapse of 30 days.
       3. Unavailability of Deponent.
   (b) Original answers not retained.
   (c) Changes do not accompany original answers.
   (d) No reasons given for changes.
2. Motions to Re-open examination, if
   (a) Changes render original examination useless, or
   (b) Changes render original examination incomplete.
3. Use of Change at trial
   (a) Impeachment as with any change.
   (b) Cross-examination of reasons for change.
   (c) Cross-examination as to persons who formulated the changes.

Form 7–6

Deposing Party's Motion to Strike Changes

Plaintiff

        v.   No._____

Defendant

[*Deposing Party's*] Motion to Strike Deposition Changes,
or in the Alternative to Re-open Examination

NOW COMES [*Deposing Party*] and moves this court pursuant to Federal Rule of Civil Procedure 30(e) to strike the changes made on the deposition transcript of [*Deponent*], or in the alternative to re-open the examination. In support of its motion [*Deposing Party*] states as follows:

1. On _____, [*Deposing Party*] took the deposition of [*Deponent*].

2(a). Upon completion of the deposition, [*Deponent*] expressly waived any right which he had to read, examine and sign the deposition transcript.

2(b). [*Deponent*] failed to sign the deposition transcript within 30 days from the date on which it was submitted to him, causing the officer before whom the examination was taken to sign on his behalf.

3. Nonetheless, [*Deponent*] has made numerous changes to his initial response to deposition questions.

4(a). Such changes are procedurally defective because they were made after [*the deponent*] effectively waived signature.

4(b). Such changes are procedurally defective because they are not stated next to the original responses on the deposition transcript.

4(c). Such changes are procedurally defective because they do not retain the original responses.

4(d). Such changes are procedurally defective because no reasons for the changes are given.

5. [Even if such changes are procedurally adequate], the reasons provided for the changes are without any legal foundation and do not justify the changes made.

6. Moreover, the changes contradict previous testimony, rendering that testimony useless and incomplete.

Wherefore [*Deposing Party*] respectfully requests this court to strike the deposition change, or at a minimum to order the deposition re-opened for a reasonable time to allow further examination regarding the changed testimony.

Respectfully Submitted,

By: _____

[NOTICE OF MOTION/FILING]
[CERTIFICATE OF SERVICE]

Form 7–7

Deposing Party's Use of Changes at Trial

Deponent:_____

Original	Tr. Pg.	Change	Reason	Impeachment/Cross-examination	Notes

Part III

THE DEFENDING PARTY'S PERSPECTIVE

Chapter 8

PREPARING FOR THE DEPOSITION

Table of Sections

---

§ 8.1   Taking an Active Role

Preparation of a witness for deposition entails the attorney's complete analysis of the case. A witness cannot be properly prepared for deposition if the lawyer has not evaluated the legal issues and the witness's position relative to those issues. The attorney should assume the witness's role in order to determine what the adversary will likely seek to bring out through questioning. Proper presentation of a deponent requires completing an investigation of the case and reviewing the significant aspects of that case with the deponent. The deponent must be prepared with the same degree of care that would be expended to prepare him to testify at trial.

Although a defending attorney may choose not to ask any questions at a deposition, his role is nevertheless an active one. The attorney must listen to all questions asked to ensure proper form and relevant inquiry. Representing the deponent requires the highest level of awareness and preparation since that attorney not only protects the information sought from the deponent, but monitors the information which may reflect the position of all parties. Information revealed at a deposition through a technically improper question may place one or more parties in a precarious or settlement-inducing position. Few attorneys likely want to be responsible for such an improper disclosure.

§ 8.2   Preparation Sessions

In the best of all worlds, an attorney will prepare a deponent for his deposition over several sessions. At the first session, the attorney should give the deponent an overview of the case, explain the deposition process, and provide him with any necessary documents for review.

During subsequent working sessions, the attorney and the deponent should study all of the documents which may be referred to by the examiner at the deposition. In addition, the attorney should recap testimony from any other witness or party who has previously been deposed or who has mentioned the current witness. The attorney should also review the witness's version of the facts in question and should critique the story to ensure its accuracy. The witness should explain the story to the attorney in narrative form to ensure that all information is consistent and accurate. Finally, the deponent's attorney should cross-examine his witness to help solidify the story and ensure its internal consistency.

The final meeting before the deposition should be a time of review. By the time of this final session, the witness should be confident with and knowledgeable of the deposition process and its relevant procedures.

Many attorneys find these time expectations excessive. Cases vary in their complexity, and depositions vary in the import of potential testimony. As such, there are often depositions for which a deponent can be prepared sufficiently in one or two fairly lengthy (two to four hours) sessions. Several preparation sessions are preferable in a complex matter, when a particular deponent plays a significant role in the litigation, or when particular deposition testimony can be inherently damaging to the case as a whole.

§ 8.3   Speaking the Deponent's Language

The preparing attorney should use common English when talking to the deponent and resist any temptation to use legalese. Many witnesses will not admit their inability to understand instructions given to them. Since the attorney spends a great deal of time preparing the witness prior to testifying to ensure that the witness's account is stated clearly, the attorney should monitor the clarity of his own language choice and style.

§ 8.4   Effective Review of the Deposition Rules

Proper preparation of a deponent necessarily includes a complete review of the general rules which govern the deposition, which often entails significant time and expense. Some attorneys attempt to reduce the time required by forwarding to the deponent through the mail a written set of deposition instructions which contain the rules of the interaction. The preparation session is then used to review those instructions.

Most deponents, however, do not understand many of the rules because they lack a frame of reference within which the rules operate. This often explains why witnesses violate the instruction not to volunteer information, and subsequently proceed to give extensive responses beyond the limited requirement of a close-ended question. It is not that the deponent failed to read the rule; it is simply that human nature fails to incorporate the adversarial nature of the interaction as an expectation. The attorney should consider having the client view a videotape of a simulated deposition designed to educate the prospective deponent about depositions.

§ 8.5 Effective Review of the Case

The deponent must understand the components of the case at issue. While some attorneys believe an unprepared deponent to be a good deponent because he will more likely need to respond with: "I don't know" to more questions, this view is fallacious. An unprepared deponent *will* disclose a host of information not known even to the presenting attorney. Therefore, reviewing all relevant information serves to highlight areas of potential danger which may arise during the interaction; such review therefore constitutes a protective measure.

Even though the attorney may have discussed the case with the client prior to the preparation session, he should review the relevant issues and update the client on any subsequently uncovered information. This refreshes the client's memory and establishes a mind-set for the deposition. Often, attorneys explain to the witness what has happened in a case, but do not explain the import of the facts. It is worth the attorney's time to review the importance of events with clients, where such exchange is protected, to provide the client with a better frame of reference for handling themselves during the deposition.

The attorney should guard any strategic disclosure with a non-client witness, because the substance of any preparation is discoverable by the other side at the deposition. Uncomfortable is a term insufficient to describe the feeling of an attorney who makes disclosures to a non-client witness because he forgets that such preparation is not protected. This warning is particularly appropriate when an attorney prepares a member of a corporate client who does not fall within the class of individuals protected by the attorney-client privilege. Such preparation is not protected and is discoverable at deposition. Thus, while the attorney should share the importance of case components with a client, a non-client should receive only that information which cannot jeopardize the party's position.

Witness preparation also includes a review of the deponent's knowledge and position. If such information has been discussed over the telephone, through the mail or in written statements prior to the deposition, the attorney should nevertheless review the deponent's story during each preparation session. Such a review refreshes the deponent's memory as to prior statements, and may jog the deponent's memory as to additional details and facts. Where a deponent lacks certain information which the attorney expected the deponent to possess, the attorney should inform the deponent as such.

Proper testimony review also includes a review of all relevant documents and tangible objects which may be presented to the witness at deposition. The pleadings, discovery responses, statements, letters, and affidavits which bear the name of the deponent or reflect on his testimony should all be reviewed prior to the deposition.

In reviewing the case with the deponent, the attorney should inform the deponent that every case has three points of view: the deponent's view, the adversary's view, and the truth. In other words, the deponent must understand that a person's testimony is tainted by his own bias or selective memory; other witnesses's view of the case will likely differ. Since all witnesses have their own personal view of the case, the deponent should not be disheartened or angered by conflicting facts or stories which arise during the interaction. The deponent should be advised to tell the truth to the best of his memory and recollection and not to worry about bringing his own story into accord with other versions presented during the deposition.

§ 8.6 Forecasting the Nature of the Deposition Interaction

The preparing attorney should explain to the deponent the nature of the deposition interaction, including varying styles of examining attorneys, the type of questions which may be employed and the scope of the questions that are likely to be asked.

There is probably no better way to explain deposition interaction than putting the deponent through a simulated deposition. The attorney may enlist the assistance of a colleague to play the role of the presenting attorney while the preparing attorney plays the role of examiner. Asking a series of questions helps the deponent to understand the nature of the interaction rules and his own testimony. Most important, the deponent can review difficult or conflicting areas of the case to ensure a clear story.

The simulated interaction should occur well in advance of the deposition itself. When the exercise occurs too close to the deposition, the deponent is prone to short term memory or hindering fear. The attorney should, whenever possible and certainly in complex or important cases, videotape the simulated interaction and review the videotape with the deponent. Lay deponents are simply too nervous to integrate too much information or analysis just prior to their deposition.

§ 8.7   Effective Review of Deposition Interaction Rules

Prior to understanding the particulars of the testimony to be given, the deponent must understand that deposition interaction operates under rules different from normal conversation. The language choice employed both in preparation and in the deposition is an important consideration because language will be the means by which the deponent constructs a picture of his testimony.

The questions asked will often distort and manipulate the manner in which information is elicited. For example, people shown a film of an auto accident and then asked implicative questions (example: Did you see *THE* broken headlight?) were more likely to report having seen something, whether or not it was actually in the film viewed prior to questioning, than were the subjects who were asked disjunctive questions (example: Did you see *A* broken headlight?). Question form affects not only the answers given by subjects, but also the representations made from their own memory. For example, people gave higher estimates of automobile speed rate when asked: "About how fast were the cars going when they *smashed* into each other?" as opposed to "About how fast were the cars going when they *hit* each other?" Even when biased questions do not affect the particular testimony, they can affect the jurors' reconstruction of the presented testimony.

The importance of language choice, style and usage in the creation of testimony in preparation of the witness cannot be overemphasized. The manner in which a particular statement is presented may influence the credibility of that statement and of the witness. Attorneys should spend significant amounts of time with their witnesses to insure that appropriate language is used to relate their accounts.

§ 8.8   The Key Rules of the Interaction

Once the witness understands the nature of the deposition, the attorney should discuss the specific rules employed in the interaction. These rules ideally should be provided to the deponent in writing prior to the deposition. The witness should also be informed that his attorney will be present for the entire deposition to ensure that only proper questions are asked. The deponent need understand that a court reporter will be present to record all of the testimony. Further, the witness should know that each party in the lawsuit will be represented by an attorney, all of whom may ask questions if they so desire. While no judge or jury is present during a deposition, the deponent must understand that the import of his testimony will surface at the time of trial, thereby reflecting on his own credibility. His testimony may also bear upon the potential for settlement of the case.

Whether or not the attorney provides the deponent with a list of rules prior to the preparation session, he should review all of the interaction rules prior to the deposition. The deposition rules of the interaction fall into two groups: those which concern the substance, content and conduct of the interaction, and those which relate to the deponent's preparation for and attitude regarding the deposition.

The first category includes rules which relate to the actual gathering, probing and evaluation of information by the examining attorney. The deponents should be reminded to:

1. Answer only the question asked; do not volunteer any additional information beyond the scope of the question, and do not expand on any previously answered question or seek to educate the examiner.

2. Answer in full, complete sentences.

3. Not guess on any answer, but state only what is actually recalled first-hand. If a specific date, time or place cannot be recalled, then the best approximation should be given, or the deponent should answer "I don't know" or "I don't recall."

4. Summarize where possible when answering a series of questions. So much better if the adversary accepts the summary.

5. Avoid all adjectives and superlatives.

6. Not tip off the examiner as to the existence of documents he does not know about.

7. Beware of questions with double negatives in them.

8. Not testify as to what others know.

9. Not testify as to a state of mind.

10. Not let the examiner testify for the deponent.

11. Not admit understanding a compound question unless there is an understanding of all parts of the question.

12. Pay attention to leading questions, which are those that suggest their own answer.

13. Not adopt the examiner's summary.

14. Take time in answering each question, and think before responding. This gives the deponent's attorney sufficient time to formulate any objections.

15. Not answer a question that is not understood; in this event, the deponent should ask for a re-wording or rephrasing of the question.

16. Not explain the thought process used to formulate a response.

17. Make it clear whether the response is a paraphrase or a direct quotation, where appropriate.

18. Look at all relevant documentation before answering any questions.

19. Not get upset over an inconsistency in responses which may arise, as every witness makes mistakes. Rehabilitation can be performed.

20. Listen to all objections. The deponent should not respond to a question when an objection has been stated by his attorney. The deponent should await the resolution of the objection.

All of these rules affect the gathering and evaluating of deposition testimony pursued by the examining attorney. Rare is the deponent who knowingly violates these rules. Rather, violations commonly occur because deponents often forget the adversarial nature of the deposition. The source of this problem may be an insufficient or undeveloped understanding of the deposition process in the preparation sessions. The presenting attorney must connect the above rules to the underlying adversarial nature of the interaction. For example, the deponent must understand that where the examining attorney fails to question on certain issues or facts perhaps deemed to be important by the deponent, it is not the duty of the deponent to bring these issues into the record. If the deponent's attorney needs such information developed, he or she will do so at the conclusion of the examiner's questioning.

Form 8–1, Witness Preparation—Relating Rules, provides the attorney with a means of relating the rules of the interaction and monitoring the clarification and explanation of these rules to the witness. Moreover, the witness should understand each of these rules and the form requires attorney notation to this effect.

The rules relating to the deponent's preparation for, and attitude concerning, the deposition process include:

1. Always tell the truth, as the deponent is sworn under oath to do so.

2.   Take the legal profession seriously; understand that a deposition is a serious proceeding and the deponent should avoid being overly friendly with the attorneys and should not be accepting of such overtures from the deposing attorney.

3.   Never pursue an argument; the attorneys are paid for that service! Always be courteous and avoid using obscenities.

4.   Wear plain, neat and comfortable clothing. The deponent should avoid heavy facial make-up and costume jewelry.

5.   Use recesses to talk in private with counsel.

6.   Remember that answers often serve to score points for the other side.

7.   Remember that there is no such thing as "off the record."

8.   If possible, never release information until there is an opportunity to go over it with counsel.

These rules advise the deponent that his or her conduct during the deposition is important. The deponent must be courteous and maintain a formal atmosphere. Similarly, permitting the deponent to become friendly with the examining attorney may lead to a violation of conduct rules, such as volunteering information.

These attitude-oriented rules are often not explained to the deponent within the framework of the interaction. For example, the deponent should understand that he must be perceived as honest and credible by the examiner and should take this point into consideration when selecting his attire. Similarly, while the "adversary as enemy" framework is often touched upon by attorneys in preparation, the attorney must express to the deponent that excessive cooperation can lead to volunteered information, thereby jeopardizing the case position. The deponent should not be thrown or made uncomfortable if asked whether he was prepared by his attorney prior to the deposition. This question is entitled to a truthful response. There is no reason for a deponent not to disclose the fact that he or she was prepared for the deposition, although substantive content of the preparation session between attorney and client is privileged. This issue is best addressed in the preparation session, preparing the deponent for questions in this regard. Moreover, the deponent should understand that although "off the record" discussions appear to be safe, any information divulged "off the record" may serve to strengthen the adversary's position.

Attorneys must further express to their clients the complexity of the deposition interaction. First, the the client needs to understand that his role is a difficult one. Second, the attorney should explain his protective role in the deposition, *i.e.*, an attorney protects his client deponent through the use of objections. The use of objections assists the attorney to monitor and control the interaction so as to ensure that only proper questions are asked. The attorney has the right to instruct the witness not to answer questions which seem unfair or improper. The attorney or witness may also request a break in the interaction to consult about a question or the direction of the testimony. The presenting attorney also protects the deponent by asking a series of questions at the end of the examiner's questioning deemed to be necessary to clarify or rehabilitate the deponent.

Regardless of the nature and extent of preparation and emphasis of the rules, no rehearsal sufficiently reflects the actual tension or dynamics of the live deposition proceeding. The attorney must judge the amount of preparation needed on both a case by case basis and a deponent by deponent basis. Some deponents will require more preparation than others to ensure adherence to the deposition rules. Since these rules are designed to protect not only the deponent, but the position of each party in the interaction by insuring proper disclosure, effective preparation is essential.

§ 8.9 Avoid Powerless Language

Deponent language choice is further highlighted by the distinction between powerful or powerless speech. "Powerless" speech is characterized by a frequent use of intensifiers (example: "so," "very," "too"), empty adjectives (example: "charming," "cute"), hyper-correct grammar, polite forms, gestures, hedges (example: "well," "you know," "I guess"), rising intonation, and a wider range of intonation patterns, *i.e.*, rising questioning intonation in a declarative context. Users of this powerless speech are generally given a negative evaluation by the receivers of such communication.

The absence of these powerless characteristics produces more forceful language which is referred to as "powerful speech." The use of powerless speech can be found in the testimony of both male and female deponents. Professionals (such as doctors, law enforcement agents, etc.) tend to use powerless speech less frequently than do people who are less educated or of lower social status. Nevertheless, powerful speech enhances the credibility of witnesses regardless of their education or social status. Therefore, the attorney should pay close attention to the words employed by that deponent to ensure a presence of clarity, assuredness, and power.

§ 8.10 Client vs. Non-client Deponents

The preparation of a non-client deponent differs from the preparation of a client. The attorney may not render legal advice or pursue matters which may conflict with his client's interests in the litigation. It is not necessary for the attorney to instruct the witness on deposition behavior since the non-client owes no allegiance to the attorney and may obtain counsel of his own. Most important, because such attorney-non-client interaction is discoverable, caution must be used in any conversation with a non-client.

§ 8.11 Witness Self–Evaluation

Preparing the non-expert witness entails not only evaluation by the presenting attorney, but self-evaluation by the witness as well. Prior to meeting with the witness for deposition preparation, the attorney may send to the witness Forms 8–2 and 8–3. Form 8–2, entitled Witness Preparation—Witness Self-Information Form, enables the witness to be prepared for deposition. It helps clarify what information the witness knows with regard to specific issues supplied by the presenting attorney. By specifying what he knows for sure, how and why he knows the information and what he does not know or understand about the issue will assist the attorney to properly prepare the witness for deposition. Form 8–3 permits the witness to specify a series of questions he has regarding the different factual or presentational components of the deposition. The attorney will be able to read into the answers provided by the witness and clarify the appropriate rules and procedures as part of preparation. These forms seek to provide insight from the witnesses' perspective, a perspective which most attorneys will neglect. These forms provide a means of ensuring that the witness's concerns get addressed prior to deposition.

§ 8.12 Understanding the Lay Witness

Form 8–4, entitled Preparing the Lay (Non-expert) Witness enables the attorney to gather basic information about that witness including his educational and employment background. The form seeks a summary of his knowledge and specifies the information known by that witness as related to the issues of the case. By establishing the limits on that information and the effect of the information on the case position, the presenting attorney is better able to determine what direction the deposition should, or more importantly, should not take.

Form 8–5 provides the presenting attorney with the means of monitoring the impression that the witness will make at deposition, and likely at trial. By specifying the deponent's attitudes toward litigation in general, and the case specifically, as well as the attorneys involved, Form 8–5 provides a predictive tool reflecting the witness's likely behavior. Comments on appearance and content of information regarding the case and deposition procedures provide essential insight into how this witness is likely to act during the deposition. Suggestions and techniques are specified to improve the deponent's conduct or position so as to provide both a tool of evaluation and of resolution. Form 8–5 may also be completed where the witness preparation includes videotaped rehearsal. This permits the attorney and witness to observe comments and evaluation from the live preparation simulation.

§ 8.13 The Expert Witness

Testimony produced in court is factual in nature. The opinions and conclusions which emerge from presented facts are left to the jury. Litigation often requires testimony from a person who possesses knowledge of a specialized nature. Federal Rule of Evidence 702 allows expert testimony:

> If scientific, technical, or other specialized knowledge will assist the trier of fact to understand the evidence or to determine a fact in issue, a witness qualified as an expert by knowledge, skill, experience, training or education, may testify thereto in the form of an opinion or otherwise.

The intent is that this expert will have some special knowledge or experience that will assist the jurors' understanding of a difficult subject matter or question at issue. (*See,* Schultz v. Richie, 148 Ill.App.3d 903, 102 Ill.Dec. 289, 499 N.E.2d 1069 (4th Dist.1986)).

§ 8.14 Types of Experts

The Federal Rules recognize three types of experts:

1. *Fact–Experts.* A fact expert is a person who qualifies as an expert and who has first-hand knowledge of the subject matter of the litigation. The courts treat a fact expert as an occurrence witness. An example of a fact expert is the treating physician. (*See* Fed.R.Civ.P. 26(b)(4)).

2. *Opinion Experts.* Opinion experts testify to a matter material to a claim or defense in the pending litigation and who may be expected to render an opinion within his or her expertise at trial. This expert may be a party, an employee of a party or an independent contractor. (*See* Fed.R.Civ.P. 26(b)(4)(a)(i)).

3. *Consulting Expert.* A consulting expert is one who is retained or specially employed in the anticipation of or in preparation for litigation, but will not be called at trial to render an opinion within his area of expertise. (*See* Fed.R.Civ.P. 26(b)(4)(b)).

Both fact experts and opinion experts are almost always deposed prior to trial. A party may take the deposition of all individuals who have knowledge of facts that will be admissible at trial or will lead to facts admissible at trial. Since fact experts possess knowledge of facts surrounding the occurrence, they may be deposed. (*See* Fed.R.Civ.P. 26(b)(4)). Because an opinion expert will have a great impact on the trier of fact, the Federal Rules permit the deposition of such an expert "upon motion." The deposition is essential to the effective cross-examination of a witness with specialized knowledge. (*See* Fed.R.Civ.P. 26(b)(4)(a)(i)).

A party may only take the deposition of a consulting expert, however, upon a showing of exceptional circumstances. Such circumstances may exist when it would be impracticable for the parties seeking discovery to obtain the facts or opinions on the same subject matter by other means. (*See* Fed.R.Civ.P. 26(b)(4)(b)).

§ 8.15 Information Required to Be Disclosed Regarding Experts

Under the federal system, a party may by interrogatory require any other party to provide the following information regarding testifying experts:

1. The persons whom the other party expects to call as an expert witness at trial.

2. The subject matter on which the expert is expected to testify.

3. The substance of the facts and opinions to which the expert is expected to testify.

4. A summary of the grounds for each opinion. (Fed.R.Civ.P. 26(b)(4)(a)(i)).

The most common way to determine the name of the opposing counsel's testifying expert is to ask for this information through interrogatory. Further discovery of the testifying expert by way of deposition must be requested by motion.

§ 8.16 Selecting the Expert

In selecting an expert to be used at deposition, and subsequently at trial, the attorney should consider the expert's professional background, point of view, personal characteristics, appearance and previous expert opinions rendered.

The education and background of the expert will affect his or her credibility and should be carefully evaluated prior to selection. An engineer who has been in private practice and has a record of publication and scholarly work will be more impressive than a young graduate with limited experience. The nature of the expert's experience should be evaluated since one from a research background will differ from one with a purely experiential background. No specific background is preferable, but the attorney must be aware of the nature of the potential expert's background prior to retaining the person.

Experts will maintain credibility and be easier to work with if they share the point of view of the presenting attorney. This is not to say a record of mixed positions is not desirable since it suggests the expert's objectivity and fairness. However, regardless of the capability of the expert, his evaluation of the case must produce a sincere point of view which aligns with the strategy to be presented at trial.

When selecting the witness the attorney should pay close attention to how the expert speaks, his mannerisms, gestures and his overall attitude toward the case. Whether the expert appears to be likeable and objective, though involved in the cause, will be important.

The qualifications of an expert may be impressive in and of themselves, but a poor appearance will destroy the credibility and impact of the testimony. The expert should appear professional, but translate his expertise into language which is easily understood by the jury. Expert witness preparation includes preparing the expert in this area; during the selection process, the attorney should observe whether the expert has the ability to be clear.

The attorney must understand the previous professional opinions taken by this expert in other cases. Prior writings of the expert, deposition transcripts and trial testimony should all be obtained and reviewed to learn whether the expert has, in fact, taken positions opposite to the one desired in the current case. No attorney should assume that his opponent will not investigate the prior testimonial record of the expert. Credibility can easily be destroyed if it is impeached by prior testimony at the time of the trial. A balanced viewpoint suggests objectivity. An expert who testifies for both defense and plaintiff positions therefore may be desirable so long as no contradiction between prior positions and the current opinions exists.

§ 8.17 Preparation Session for the Expert Deponent

Preparing the expert witness is substantially similar to preparing the lay witness. All of the interaction rules for the lay witness are applicable to the expert.

The essential difference in preparation of an expert from a lay witness rests in the likely prior experience of the expert. Unlike the lay witness, whom the attorney has probably met for the first or second time, the expert is often a familiar figure since he or she is used in several cases of the same nature. As a result, preparation of the expert may be routine. Nevertheless, if this is the first preparation session for the expert, then all rules should be reviewed. If the expert is known to be experienced and capable, many of the traditional rules are often reviewed quickly and without significant depth. However, there are other elements which must be reviewed with the expert prior to deposition.

It is imperative that the expert review the subject matter upon which he will testify at deposition. This includes acquiring and reviewing all relevant records, looking at documents located in the files and reading all relevant books, articles and treatises on the subject. The attorney should review all the information entertained by the expert that is likely set out in a written report to the attorney. While the attorney is not the expert in the matter, all attorneys seek to develop a level of expertise so they understand the technical concepts presented at deposition and trial. The attorney and expert should review together all academic and case-specific information.

The attorney should also review the background of the expert, the area of expertise and extent of testimonial experience. Preparation for the session includes a review of the expert's curriculum vitae and prior transcripts. The attorney should review this information with the expert to clarify in their relationship that the presenting attorney is well aware of the expert's prior testifying record.

The attorney should review related jury instructions with the expert witness so that the expert understands the law applicable to the case and the necessary direction of the testimony. This can affect the manner of presentation by that witness.

Thus, the preparation of an expert witness is handled on a somewhat higher level than that of a lay witness. The expert understands the procedures and strategy of the deposition and should be treated as such. It is, nevertheless, important for the attorney to maintain control over the information presented and the direction in which the testimony flows. The preparation session will assist to develop and maintain that control.

§ 8.18　Understanding the Expert Witness

Preparing the expert witness entails a different approach because the expert is retained for specific purpose and issue. *See* Form 8–6. The form specifies the issues involving the expert, seeks the background information of the expert, but then clarifies the opinions and basis for each such opinion. Combined with the sections related to appearance and overall content and attitude, Form 8–6 provides a meaningful way for the presenting attorney to monitor the appearance and effect of his expert.

§ 8.19　Monitoring the Interaction

Form 8–7 provides a means for the protecting attorney to specify the testimony and clarify whether any follow-up is needed. Form 8–8 allows the attorney to monitor the issues being raised, the specific questions and answers and whether any objections were registered. The protecting attorney is provided a clear means of the propriety of the examiner's conduct by monitoring the need for and execution of objections.

Form 8–9, Maintaining Relations at the Deposition, complements Forms 8–7 and 8–8 by predicting the atmosphere of the deposition. Moreover, the protecting attorney cites means of creating or avoiding particular working atmospheres specified on the form, in the form of specific tactics and hindering factors.

After the completion of the deposition, the protecting attorney must evaluate the deposition. Forms 8–10 and 8–11 provide post-evaluation by having the attorney specify the issue, testimony related, implications of the testimony and necessary follow-up, as well as witness evaluations. Other discovery procedures may be required to clear up any resultant confusion or to advance the case for settlement or trial.

Form 8–1

Witness Preparation—Relating Rules

Case _____ File _____ Client _____

Deponent Name: _____

Rule	Stated	Explained	Witness Comprehends (through repetition or example)
1. understands question			
2. answers only the question asked			
3. be responsive			
4. keep answer simple			
5. maintain independence			
6. no volunteering			
7. be confident			
8. say "I do not know" when needed			
9. be certain to hear question			
10. do not be cut off			
11. keep answers verbal			
12. answers given assume understood question			
13. request a break when needed			
14. supplement answer when necessary			
15. observe objections as a cue to be aware of the question or answer to which the objection refers			
16. observe nonverbal cues/signals directed to questions or answers			

When completed, see if there are any questions still existing in the witness's mind. Give the witness as many examples as possible to clarify each rule.

Form 8–2

Witness Preparation—Witness Self–Information Form

Directions: The following form is designed to help you be a better witness at deposition. Human nature encourages us to often say things we cannot be certain of in order to help out. In the deposition, it is essential we say no more than what is asked of us—this form will help you clarify for yourself what you know or do not know. The specific topic or issue has been specified by your attorney.

Complete this form on your own or with the assistance of your attorney, but be certain to review your answers with your attorney before testifying at the deposition.

Issue # 1 (to be filled in by the attorney): _____

What I know for sure about this issue: _____

_____

_____

_____

How I know what I am certain I know: _____

_____

_____

_____

Why I know what I know for sure: _____

_____

_____

_____

What I do not know (and therefore could not testify to) about this issue: _____

_____

_____

_____

What I do not understand about this issue: _____

_____

_____

_____

Issue # 2 (to be filled in by the attorney): _____

What I know for sure about this issue: _____

_____

_____

_____

How I know what I am certain I know: _____

_____

_____

_____

Why I know what I know for sure: _____

_____

_____

_____

What I do not know (and therefore could not testify to) about this issue: _____

_____

_____

_____

What I do not understand about this issue: _____

_____

_____

_____

Form 8–2 (continued)

Form 8–3

Witness Preparation—Witness Question Sheet

Directions: This form is designed to let you think about some of the questions you may want to ask the attorney. This form enables you to analyze your thoughts.

1. Questions I have concerning the facts of this case: _____

_____

_____

_____

_____

2. Questions I have concerning how to answer questions properly: _____

_____

_____

_____

_____

3. Questions I have concerning how to dress/appear at the deposition: _____

_____

_____

_____

4. Questions I have concerning the atmosphere of the deposition: _____

_____

_____

_____

_____

5. Questions I have concerning the procedures of the deposition: _____

_____

_____

_____

6. Questions I have concerning how I may interact with the attorneys: _____

_____

_____

_____

7. Questions I have concerning how I act when an objection is made by an attorney: _____

_____

_____

_____

You should give significant consideration to these questions and be certain to discuss these matters with your attorney until all questions have been answered in your mind.

Form 8–4

Preparing the Lay (Non-expert) Witness

Case_____ File_____ Client_____

Deponent Name: _____

Address: _____

_____

Telephone: _____

Scheduled Deposition Date: _____

Date of Witness Preparation: _____

Preparation Time: From_____ To_____

1. Relevant Personal Information:

    A. Previous address(es)_____

    _____

    B. Occupation: _____

    C. Employer: _____

    D. Birthdate: _____

    E. Social Security Number: _____

    F. Marital Status: _____

    G. Children (name, age, and addresses): _____

    _____

    _____

    H. Educational Background: _____

    _____

    _____

    _____

I.   Previous Employment Record: _____

_____

_____

_____

_____

2.   Summary of Witness knowledge: _____

_____

_____

_____

_____

_____

_____

_____

3.   Specific Information Known:

Issue	Fact Known	Basis of Knowledge	Supporting Evidence	Effect on Case Position	Limits on Info

Form 8–4 (continued)

Comments: _____

_____

_____

_____

_____

Form 8–5

Witness Preparation—Impression Maintenance

Case _____ File _____ Client _____

Deponent: _____   Date of Preparation _____

1. Specify the Deponent's attitude towards Litigation: _____

    _____

    _____

    _____

    _____

2. Specify the Deponent's attitude towards this case: _____

    _____

    _____

    _____

    _____

3. Specify the Deponent's attitude towards the presenting attorney: _____

    _____

    _____

    _____

    _____

4. Specify the Deponent's attitude towards attorneys in general: _____

    _____

    _____

    _____

    _____

5. Appearance: (appropriateness of dress, conduct, grooming)

    Strengths: _____

    _____

    _____

Weaknesses: _____

_____

_____

Ways to Improve: _____

_____

_____

6. Content: (information related, preparedness, how information is related, understanding of procedures, ability to understand directions, control over testimony)

Regarding the Case:

Strengths: _____

_____

_____

Weaknesses: _____

_____

_____

Ways to Improve: _____

_____

_____

Regarding Deposition Procedure:

Strengths: _____

_____

_____

Weaknesses: _____

_____

_____

Ways to Improve: _____

_____

_____

Form 8–5 (continued)

7. Attitude: (deponent's relation with the attorneys, others present)

Regarding the Case:

Strengths: _____

_____

_____

Weaknesses: _____

_____

_____

Ways to Improve: _____

_____

_____

Regarding Deposition Procedure:

Strengths: _____

_____

_____

Weaknesses: _____

_____

_____

Ways to Improve: _____

_____

_____

8. Specific suggestions related to deponent for improvement: _____

_____

_____

_____

9. Specific techniques needed to improve deponent's position (document review, another preparation session, etc.): _____

_____

_____

_____

Form 8–5 (continued)

Form 8–6

Preparing the Expert Witness

Case _____ File _____ Client _____

Deponent's Name: _____

Title or Profession: _____

Address: _____

_____

_____

Telephone: _____

Scheduled Date of Deposition _____

Date of Preparation Session _____

Time of Preparation: From _____ To _____

Issue for which this expert has been retained: _____

_____

1. Relevant Background Information:

   a. education: (degrees, schools attended, certificates, licenses)

   _____

   _____

   _____

   b. work history: (positions and chronology)

   _____

   _____

   _____

   _____

   _____

   _____

   _____

c. honors:

_____

_____

_____

d. publications: (title, year and name of publication)

_____

_____

_____

_____

_____

_____

e. prior testimony given as expert: (case name, side represented, issues addressed, and case outcome)

_____

_____

_____

_____

2. Summary of Opinions in this case: _____

_____

_____

3. Specify *Opinion # 1:* _____

_____

_____

a. basis for opinion: _____

_____

_____

b. supporting information for opinion: _____

_____

_____

c. contradictory information: _____

_____

_____

_____

d. limits on opinion: _____

_____

_____

_____

e. opposition's likely position relative to opinion: _____

_____

_____

_____

Specify *Opinion # 2:* _____

_____

_____

_____

a. basis for opinion: _____

_____

_____

b. supporting information for opinion: _____

_____

_____

c. contradictory information: _____

_____

_____

d. limits on opinion: _____

_____

_____

e. opposition's likely position relative to opinion: _____

_____

Specify *Opinion # 3:* _____

_____

_____

a. basis for opinion: _____

_____

_____

b. supporting information for opinion: _____

_____

_____

c. contradictory information: _____

_____

_____

d. limits on opinion: _____

_____

_____

e. opposition's likely position relative to opinion: _____

_____

_____

4. Work necessary to further strengthen the opinion(s): _____

_____

_____

_____

_____

_____

Form 8–6 (continued)

5. Appearance: (appropriateness of dress, conduct, grooming)

Strengths: _____

_____

_____

Weaknesses: _____

_____

_____

Ways to Improve: _____

_____

_____

6. Relating content: (effectiveness, preparedness, clarity, control over testimony, verbosity and responsiveness)

Strengths: _____

_____

_____

Weaknesses: _____

_____

_____

Ways to Improve: _____

_____

_____

7. Attitude: (relations with attorney, others present)

Strengths: _____

_____

_____

Weaknesses: _____

_____

_____

Form 8–6 (continued)

Ways to Improve: _____

_____

_____

8. Specific suggestions related to improve overall presentation: _____

_____

_____

_____

Form 8–7

Monitoring Interaction

Case _____ File _____ Client _____

Deponent: _____

Deponent's Testimony	Follow Up Needed?	Specify	Comments
1.			
2.			
3.			
4.			
5.			
6.			
7.			
8.			
9.			
10.			

Form 8–8

Protecting the Deponent

Case _____ File _____ Client _____

Deponent Name: _____

Issue	Area of Questioning	Question	Answer	Objection?	Comments (Follow up)

Form 8–9

Maintaining Relations at the Deposition

Other Attorneys Present:

Name	Firm Name	Client
_____	_____	_____
_____	_____	_____
_____	_____	_____

1. Personality Profile Summary:

Name	Preparation	Legal Analysis Competent?	Attitude
_____	_____	_____	_____
_____	_____	_____	_____
_____	_____	_____	_____
_____	_____	_____	_____

2. Overall, the interaction in this deposition is likely to be:

____Comfortable ____Uncomfortable ____Neutral

____Positive   ____Negative

____Shared   ____Dominated by: _____

_____

3. I wish to create a ____cordial/cooperative ____adversarial atmosphere.

4. I can help create the desired atmosphere by: _____

_____

_____

5. Tactics to employ to insure the desired atmosphere: _____

_____

_____

6. Factors which may hinder the desired atmosphere: _____

_____

_____

7. Tactics to employ to *counteract* hindrances: _____

_____

_____

Form 8–10

Post–Deposition Evaluation Form

Case _____ File _____ Client _____

Deponent: _____

Issue	Testimony	Implications	Need Follow up

Form 8–11

Post–Deposition Deponent Evaluation

Case _____ File _____ Client _____

Deponent: _____

Date of Deposition: _____

Summary of Testimony: _____

_____

Directions: Rate each of the following as *Excellent, Good, Average, Fair,* or *Poor* (Needs significant work)

1. Witness Evaluation: *Content*

   a. Consistency of Testimony   _____

   b. Coherency of Testimony   _____

   c. Completeness of Testimony   _____

   d. Logical Presentation   _____

   e. Clarity of Presentation   _____

2. Witness Evaluation: *Presentation*

   a. Kept responses brief   _____

   b. Was not verbose   _____

   c. Followed lead of presenting attorney   _____

   d. Appeared confident   _____

   e. Presented favorable disposition   _____

   f. Spoke fluently   _____

3. Overall, if this deponent was called to testify at trial, the appearance of this deponent as a witness would be:

   ___ Excellent ___ Good ___ Average ___ Fair ___ Poor

4. Case and witness evaluation lead me to conclude that we

   ___ Must call   ___ Should not call   ___ Must not call

   ___ Should call   ___ May need to call   ___ Will not likely need this witness.

Form 8–11

5. Pretrial Follow-up

   a.   further preparation of this witness needed: _____

       _____

       _____

       _____

       _____

   b.   review the following documents: _____

       _____

       _____

       _____

   c.   review the following documents with the witness: _____

       _____

       _____

       _____

   d.   depose the following people: _____

       _____

       _____

   e.   send written interrogatories to: _____

       _____

       _____

       On issue of: _____

       _____

       _____

   f.   prepare requests to admit to: _____

       _____

       On issue of: _____

       _____

Form 8–11 (continued)

6. Other Comments: _____

    _____

    _____

    _____

    _____

Chapter 9

PRESENTING THE DEPONENT

Table of Sections

----

§ 9.1 Protecting the Deponent

Protecting a deponent means guarding the client's best interests in the deposition in accordance with the customs, practices and rules of the interaction. Protecting the client requires objecting to violations of procedural or substantive rules. In addition, presenting attorneys have the right to obstruct questioning for a legitimate purpose. They may have questions repeated by a court reporter if they do not hear or are confused by a question. They may examine documents handed to the client before questions are asked or insist upon a break in the interaction where the deponent appears confused or tired. Where the client requests a conference, the presenting attorney may confer with the client so long as a question is not pending. Where the deponent has misstated information or is heading on a dangerous route, the presenting attorney may interrupt and warn the deponent. Deponents who go beyond the questions asked may be reminded that they have "answered the question and need not go beyond." All of these protective devices should be used when necessary.

Attorneys frequently employ tactics other than objections, such as specifying testimony for the record, whispering privately in the deponent's ear, sending a non-verbal signal (such as a facial gesture or kick under the table) or demanding numerous breaks in the interaction. These tactics, if repeated, unnecessarily may be found abusive or in bad faith resulting in sanctions.

§ 9.2 Establishing a Role

Many attorneys assume the presentation of a deponent to be a passive role. These attorneys seek to remain in the background of the interaction, allowing the examiner to control the direction. This posture is erroneous. Representing a deponent is an essential function of the deposition process requiring the lawyer to take an active role. The protecting attorney must ensure that all questions asked by the examiner are of proper form and directed to relevant areas. The adversarial nature of the deposition requires the attorney to object to rule violations.

The presenting attorney who ensures that all rules are followed and objects at every violation is the "diligent enforcer." This attorney, formal in approach, argues with every examiner who rejects his objections. These attorneys establish their protector role in no uncertain terms they are eager to exhibit. Conversely, the "friendly enforcer" calls attention to some or all violations, but in a seemingly cooperative manner. These attorneys seem more interested in maintaining a cooperative atmosphere than they do in controlling the shape of the interaction. As such, they often do not object to a violation unless it is important to the interaction.

A deponent's attorney may start out as a "diligent enforcer" to establish his presence in the deposition, but shift to a more friendly role once the examiner appears to follow the rules. A shift to a diligent role from a cooperative stance serves as a signal of caution to the examiner that he adhere to interaction guidelines.

The protecting attorney forms a team with the deponent. This team works together to signal unclear or otherwise loaded questions. The protecting attorney must ensure that deponent answers are based on first-hand recollection.

§ 9.3 Functions of the Presenting Attorney

When representing a deponent or attending depositions of non-client deponents, the attorney should:

(1) monitor the propriety of the interaction;

(2) make timely objections;

(3) instruct the deponent not to answer when appropriate;

(4) use strategic objections; and

(5) decide when to rehabilitate the deponent.

§ 9.4 Monitoring the Propriety of Interaction

Nonexamining attorneys monitor and control the propriety of the interaction by raising objections when necessary during the deposition. Federal Rule 32(d) describes the situations which necessitate an objection during the deposition.

A. *Errors in Deposition Notice.* Subsection 1 of Rule 32(d) states that errors and irregularities in the deposition notice will be waived unless a written objection is properly served upon the party who gave the notice. This Rule precludes a party who fails to appear at a deposition from relying on a technical defect. It is important to note that not all errors may give rise to this requirement; listing an incorrect date or location, for example, would not necessarily be an error if the other party or deponent had been notified of the changed time or location.

B. *Disqualification of Examiner.* Subsection 2 of the Rule states that any objection based upon the disqualification of the officer who will take the deposition will be waived unless made before the taking of the deposition begins, or as soon as the disqualification becomes known, or could have been discovered, through reasonable diligence.

C. *Objecting to the Competency, Relevancy or Materiality of Testimony.* Objections to the competencey, relevancy or materiality of testimony are not waived by a failure to make such objections before or during the deposition, unless the basis for the objection is one that might have been eliminated if presented at the time of the deposition. Fed.R.Civ. P. 32(d)(3)(A). The Federal Rules eliminate immateriality as an objection, and while relevancy and competency objections are available, only the former is commonly used.

The relevancy objection is guided by Fed.R.Civ.P. 26. The scope of relevance under this rule is much more liberal than the scope of relevance under Federal Rule of Evidence 401. As such, deposition questions seeking information that may not be relevant or admissible at trial are common and proper during discovery; the protecting attorney must nevertheless define those questions which are irrelevant, even under the broad scope of Fed.R.Civ.P. 26.

D. *Other Irregularities.* Irregularities regarding the taking of the deposition, oath or affirmation, conduct of the parties or "errors of any kind which might be obviated, removed or cured if promptly presented" will be waived unless made "seasonably" at the time of deposition. Fed.R.Civ.P. 32(d)(3)(B). An attorney who believes he can sidestep the impact of testimony, because the deponent had not been sworn, will be precluded from raising this objection later since seasonable notice and available opportunity existed at the time of deposition which would have removed or cured this error.

The seasonable standard also requires that objections to the form of questions and answers be made at the time of the examination. Where questions could be modified at the time of objection, the presenting attorney must register an objection and permit a cure. This objection refers to problems of question and form such as ambiguity, complexity, confusing, or otherwise inappropriate questions. The standard would also reflect non-responsive answers.

Some aggressive presenting attorneys will object when they hear leading questions during the deposition. This response is inappropriate; the deponent is often adverse to the examiner permitting the use of leading questions. The presenting attorney is advised to recognize a distinction between appropriately used leading questions and improper argumentative or hostile questions.

§ 9.5 Timing of Objections

The protecting attorney must register objections to questions at the time of deposition. Failure to do so will result in the waiver of such rights. The client will be bound by the attorney's failure to raise objections in a timely manner. For example, an attorney who fails to object to questions regarding privileged matter will waive such objections after the deposition. Attempts to resolve the matter at trial will fail since the waiver occurred during the deposition. Attorneys often attempt to protect all individuals involved by stipulating that objections to questions and answers would be reserved by each party, except for objections reflecting the form of the question. Attorneys are cautioned that a judge may not recognize such an agreement and may simply resort to the governing rules as determinative.

§ 9.6 Instructing the Deponent Not to Answer

Since in most cases registering an objection at deposition will be sufficient to preclude the information from coming in at the time of trial as impeachment, most questions will be answered at deposition subject to the objection. However, there are times when an attorney will register an objection and instruct the deponent not to answer the question. Instructions not to answer a deposition question are proper only in two situations: where the information sought is privileged or where the question is harassing. An instruction not to answer is not proper based on the irrelevance of the question. *See, e.g.,* Ralston Purina Company v. McFarland, 550 F.2d 967, 973 (4th Cir.1977).

§ 9.7 Deciding to Instruct Not to Answer

In deciding whether to instruct the witness not to answer, attorneys strike a balance between the inconvenience of that witness's disclosure of information which will be precluded at trial based upon objection at deposition and the harm caused by having to reconvene the deposition to get information determined to be appropriate. (W.R. Grace & Company v. Pullman, Inc., 74 F.R.D. 80, 84 (W.D.Okla.1977)).

Protecting attorneys must remember that they have no right to instruct a non-client deponent not to answer a question. The protecting attorney may make a suggestion to the witness that such a question is likely inappropriate and need not be answered. The non-client witness, however, will make such a decision based on his own judgment. Non-client witnesses thus may attend a deposition with their own attorney present. In fact, the protecting attorney may be violating an ethical disciplinary rule by advising a non-client deponent in a legal way other than encouraging that deponent to seek legal representation. (See, Code of Professional Responsibility DR7–104(2)).[1]

---

1. "During the course of his representation of a client, a lawyer shall not . . . . 2. Give advice to a person who is not represented by a lawyer, other than the advice to secure counsel, if the interests of such person are or have a reasonable possibility of being in conflict with the interests of his client."

§ 9.8 Responding to an Instruction Not to Answer

The examiner may respond to an instruction not to answer a question in two ways. First, the attorney may simply drop the issue and move on. Second, the attorney may turn to the deponent and ask whether that person will answer the question or not, based on the advice of his attorney. Where the examiner seems to create an interference by beginning to explain implications of certifying questions based upon objection, the presenting attorney is urged to step in and limit the examiner's lectures. Failure to do this may make uncomfortable the deponent who fears personal implications. The protecting attorney should be aware that the examiner may nevertheless attempt to repeat the question in a different form or at a different time or may work to discuss, on or off the record, the need to have the question answered. The presenter may stick by his decision, but must have a legitimate basis for preventing disclosure.

§ 9.9 Objections as Strategy

There are times when a protecting attorney will register an objection for reasons other than a rule violation, based on strategy. An objection can often disrupt the train of thought of an examiner who may not pursue an answer after an objection is registered. The examiner may see his own question as improper and fear admitting that he sees the problem. There may be times when the examiner is not sure of the propriety of the question being asked, and an objection made at the right time may be sufficient to shift the approach of the examiner.

The mere registering of objections is usually seen by the deponent as a signal that something is wrong with the question or subsequent answer. Clients are best advised during deposition preparation that the registering of an objection should be seen as a signal that encourages them to maintain guard at that time.

Any non-examining attorney has the right to register objections to any questions posed to a deponent, whether or not that deponent is a client. The objection may cause the examiner to lose his train of thought, or even to become argumentative. The objection thus may destroy the rapport which the examiner is trying to build.

Protecting attorneys should nevertheless be aware that registering an objection can induce an attorney to seek even more information than originally intended. For example, where objection is made to question form, the examiner may respond by asking a series of foundational or otherwise probing questions to establish the relevancy of the question or suggest why the form may be proper. As such, even more detailed information than was originally sought will come of record, all of which could have been avoided by not registering the objection to the initial question. Therefore, protecting attorneys must consider the negative implications of registering objections.

§ 9.10 Rehabilitation—Questioning the Deponent

When determining whether questions of one's own client should be asked, an attorney must exercise restraint. Any questions asked by the protecting attorney create a risk of additional disclosure. Furthermore, the deponent cannot be expected to respond in a desirable manner. The examiner therefore takes a risk as to what answers will be given. In general, the protecting attorney who asks questions sends signals to the examiner that further information is out there to be gathered.

§ 9.11 When Rehabilitation Is Appropriate

There will be times when rehabilitative questions should be asked. For example, where the deponent will not be available for trial due to death, illness, absence from the jurisdiction of the court or otherwise, the only available testimony will be deposition testimony. As such, certain important information must be established. At other times, the examining attorney may have not permitted the deponent to render complete answers on the record. The protecting attorney may seek to permit such clarification or supplementation prior to the termination of the deposition. Where a deponent has misstated information or neglected to provide important information, the protecting attorney may seek to have such information on the record for purposes of accuracy or completeness. Where the protecting attorney seeks to settle the litigation, it is desirable to bring certain testimony of record which will assist in the settlement posture.

§ 9.12 When Rehabilitation Is Inappropriate

The client deponent is a favorable witness. It should not be the intention of the protecting attorney to ensure that all relevant information has been placed on the record. Where an examiner fails, for whatever reason, to gather the entire story from the deponent, such tactical error need not be corrected by the protecting attorney. In such cases, the protecting attorney, who desires to bring information into the record simply because the examiner neglected to do so, makes the same grave error deponents are warned against: volunteering information.

Chapter 10

NON–VERBAL COMMUNICATION IN THE DEPOSITION

Table of Sections

---

§ 10.1 The Significance of Non-verbal Cues

The non-verbal cues which accompany messages from the protecting attorney are significant. The tone of voice used by the presenting attorney to register objections or protect the deponent, and the way in which the protecting attorney controls and moves his body, all affect the atmosphere of the interaction and potential testimony of the deponent.

§ 10.2 Use of Voice

The protecting attorney should be aware that the tone of voice used when interacting with other participants in the deposition greatly shapes the interaction atmosphere.

Where the examiner steps out of bounds in questioning propriety or is otherwise hostile or unfair to the deponent, the protecting attorney can utilize an aggressive or stern vocal tone to warn the examiner to observe procedural rules. An examiner who sees that a protecting attorney means business will often modify his behavior.

Where other attorneys present at the deposition consistently register objections or can otherwise interrupt the interaction, the protecting attorney can utilize vocal tone to put them aback as well. In effect, all participants, other than the deponent, can be alerted through strong vocal tone that the protecting attorney is closely monitoring and observing the interaction to ensure adherence to the rules.

Aggressive vocal tone may be the most useful means of signaling a deponent that he is violating a procedural rule. The deponent, when volunteering information, will take heed when the attorney aggressively warns, "you've answered the question!" Some deponents need strong urging before they finally realize the error of their ways. The protecting attorney should never hesitate to use an aggressive tone when a deponent gives answers beyond the question asked, including potentially harmful information.

§ 10.3 Effective Body Language

The protecting attorney's posture affects the atmosphere and direction of the testimony. Body positioning also reflects the alertness of the protecting attorney as well. An attorney who leans back comfortably and casually will create an impression of comfort to the other participants and may become passive in his own monitoring of the interaction. Such a position may be acceptable during preliminary or background questioning, but the protecting attorney should always sit straight up to remain aware.

Even while sitting straight up, an attorney may lean forward in his chair, signalling concern and heightened attention. Such behavior can have the same effect as registering an objection; it diverts the examining attorney's direction of questioning. When combined with a stare or otherwise strong eye contact to the examiner, the attorney in an aggressively leaning forward position sends a strong signal to the examiner that questions must be appropriate or that he may be treading on inappropriate grounds.

Similarly, by leaning forward and making eye contact with the deponent, the protecting attorney sends a signal to the deponent that his answer or subsequent answers must be guarded. A deponent who is prepared during the preparation session to watch the body positioning of his attorney will pick up on the cues of caution and monitor his responses.

§ 10.4   Monitoring Personal Space

Often, the deposition is taken at the office of or location selected by the examining attorney. The presenting attorney has no control over the design or layout of the examination room. The size of the conference table, and other room artifacts, are out of the control of the presenting attorney. The attorney can do little more than attempt to structure the seating location of the participants. By sitting next to the deponent, the protecting attorney is in the best position to signal or monitor the interaction. The protecting attorney can resort to touch as a means of signaling caution to the deponent. However, sitting across from the deponent enables the attorney to use eye contact and effective posturing as signals to the deponent, who is then in straight view. Sitting next to the deponent enables the protecting attorney to consult with the deponent verbally and in confidence. Sitting across from the deponent, however, provides better non-verbal channels to signal the deponent. Since constant verbal interruptions may rise to the level of obstruction, the protecting attorney may decide to use non-verbal cues as his signal system. None of these non-verbal cues need appear on the record.

§ 10.5   Monitoring the Non-verbal Cues of Others

Aside from using non-verbal cues to control the other attorneys and the deponent, the protecting attorney should monitor the cues exercised by others. The deponent should be advised to sit up straight so as to maintain his own alertness in response. An unalert deponent is a dangerous deponent since he makes unknowing disclosures. The comfortable or cooperative positions of other attorneys provide a means of evaluating the likely direction of the interaction. A frustrated or hostile examiner is more likely to lean forward and begin pointing at a deponent, agressive cues of which the defending attorney should be aware.

§ 10.6   Making a Record

Most attorneys recognize that non-verbal signals or cues are not recorded on the transcript by the court reporter. As such, non-verbal communication provides a powerful way of controlling the interaction. The attorney should never forget his ability to place on to the record inappropriate conduct which could in itself be the basis for sanctions against the attorney utilizing such conduct. For example, a frustrated examiner who consistently pounds his fist on the table and uses an aggressive and loud tone of voice may scare a deponent into making a disclosure. While the record would not illustrate such behavior, the protecting attorney can state on the record: "Mr. Examiner, there is no need for you to pound your fist on the table and raise your tone of voice to a level which is clearly upsetting to the deponent and unsettling to myself as well." Such a statement will likely produce a swift modification in behavior by the examiner who realizes that subsequent tactics will be exposed by this observant competent attorney.

Chapter 11

DEFENDING ATTORNEY'S RIGHT TO TERMINATE THE DEPOSITION AND SEEK JUDICIAL RELIEF

Table of Sections

---

§ 11.1 Introduction

The defending attorney hopes that with the proper presentation of his witness and the proper use of objections he can manage the conflict in a deposition so as to control damage done to his client. He may even exercise enough foresight to obtain a protective order before the deposition, limiting its harmful scope.

Nonetheless, no amount of preparation can prevent all damage to the deponent. A witness can be damaged properly or improperly. The deponent who offers harmful testimony in response to proper questions has been properly damaged. The presenting attorney can only hope to limit that damage by preparation and strategic objections. But where the deponent has instead been "damaged" by improper questioning, the defending attorney must consider stronger defensive tactics. This chapter provides a road map to the presenting attorney of those tactics, from termination of the deposition to court-awarded sanctions for discovery abuse.

§ 11.2 Defending Attorney's Termination of the Deposition

At any time during a deposition, the defending attorney or the deponent may demand that the examination be suspended for a time necessary to move for a court order terminating or limiting the examination. Fed.R.Civ.P. 30(d). The motion may be made formally or by telephone. It may be raised before the court where the action is pending or where the deposition is being taken. *Id.* If the court orders the examination terminated, however, it may be re-opened only by order of the court in which the action is pending.

In order to prevail on the motion to limit or terminate examination, however, the movant must show that the examination was conducted in bad faith or in a manner so as to annoy, embarrass or oppress the deponent. Although this language suggests a heavy burden on the movant, the courts have not hesitated to grant motions to limit or terminate depositions in the following circumstances:

(1) when questioning is patently beyond the scope of discovery;

(2) where questioning is intended to invade the privacy of the witness with no probative value;

(3) where questioning creates undue expense;

(4) where questioning repeatedly concerns matters claimed to be privileged;

(5) where questioning elicits work-product materials; or

(6) where questioning has lasted unnecessarily long.

See e.g. Wright & Miller, Federal Practice and Procedure, §§ 2036–2044, 2116. The court has wide discretion to enter any order limiting the examination where appropriate.

Although the defending attorney may at any time move for an order limiting or terminating a deposition, he should do so only as a last resort. The attorney will risk annoying and oppressing the judge if the motion is not well-founded. Moreover, unless the judge orders complete termination (which is unlikely), the defending attorney's motion merely prolongs the deposition—further harassing the witness.

Finally, if the examiner insists on an improper avenue of questioning, and the defending attorney insists on an instruction not to answer, the examiner also has the right to adjourn the deposition to seek judicial relief. When questioning reaches this kind of impasse, attorneys instinctively engage in a "race" to the courthouse, or telephone, as the case may be. Rather than demonstrating their inability to act as professionals in a self-policing manner, however, the attorneys should consider reconciling their differences without judicial intervention. Alternatively, where a genuine dispute as to the propriety of questioning arises, the attorneys should dispassionately seek from the court a ruling on a controlling legal question before proceeding.

§ 11.3   Defending Attorney's Sanctions

The defending attorney has available two forms of sanctions in connection with improper deposition questioning. First, as expressly provided by Federal Rule of Civil Procedure 30(d), the defending attorney must receive the expenses incurred in successfully obtaining an order limiting or terminating a deposition, unless a reasonable attorney in the examiner's position would have opposed the motion. *See* Fed.R.Civ.P. 37(a)(4). Because most if not all examining attorneys would oppose a motion to limit or terminate their examination, the rule allows defending parties little practical hope of recovering the costs of the motion.

Second, the defending attorney can attempt to obtain sanctions under Federal Rule of Civil Procedure 11. That rule and its discovery corollary, Fed.R.Civ.P. 26(g), however, are triggered only when an attorney *signs* a document filed in court; they have no express application to abusive deposition tactics. Still, the defending attorney can argue that Rule 11 sanctions are proper because the examiner's filed and signed responses to the motion to limit or terminate the examination violate the rules. The examiner may incur Rule 11 sanctions if his deposition conduct is motivated by a purpose to harass, delay or increase the cost of litigation.

Unfortunately, however, the recovery of sanctions for abusive deposition questioning is unlikely. Instead, the defending attorney must rely on the termination of the deposition itself as the harshest sanction. An example of the defending attorney's motion to limit or terminate the deposition is included as Form 11–1.

DEFENDING ATTORNEY'S MOTION TO LIMIT OR TERMINATE

Plaintiff

     v.   No. _____

Defendant

   NOW COMES [*Deponent or moving Attorney*] and moves this court pursuant to Federal Rule of Civil Procedure 30(d) to terminate or limit the deposition of [*Deponent*] in the above matter. In support of its motion to terminate or limit, [*Deponent or Moving Attorney*] states as follows:

   1. From _____ to _____, [*examining party*] has deposed [*Deponent*].

   2. [*Examining party*] has conducted the examination in bad faith, repeatedly asking questions not reasonably calculated to lead to admissible evidence, but instead to annoy, embarrass and to oppress the deponent.

   3. Despite diligent and good faith efforts to resolve the conflict which has developed at this deposition, [*the examiner*] persists in his bad faith questioning. (*see* Tr. pgs. ___ to ___).

   4. The persistent bad faith techniques of [*the examining*] party leave [*defending attorney*] no choice but to seek a court order terminating or limiting the examination.

   5. The [*deponent*] will continue to be severely prejudiced if the deposition is allowed to proceed.

   WHEREFORE, [*moving party*] respectfully urges the court to enter an order terminating, or in the alternative, limiting the deposition of [*deponent*] in this matter.

           Respectfully submitted,

           By: _____

           [NOTICE OF MOTION/FILING]

           [CERTIFICATE OF SERVICE]

Chapter 12

DEFENDING ATTORNEY'S POST–DEPOSITION PROCEDURES

Table of Sections

---

§ 12.1 Introduction

The defending attorney's job does not end when the deposition questioning ends. The deposition testimony must first be transcribed and submitted to the deponent for examination and signature. These post-deposition procedures are not routine and should not be treated as such. Instead, if used properly, they offer the defending attorney an excellent opportunity to control any damage to the witness that might have been done during the questioning. As explained in this chapter, these post-deposition formalities are tools available to the defending attorney. Forms 12–1 and 12–2 allow the defending attorney to summarize the deposition and then ensure that each of the post-deposition procedures is used to its fullest extent.

§ 12.2 Submission of Record to Deponent

The deponent has the absolute right to:

(1) have the deposition transcribed or recorded in a readily discernable fashion;

(2) read the record or have it read to him;

(3) examine the record or have it examined for him; and

(4) make any changes whatsoever in the record before signing the record. *See e.g.* Fed.R. Civ.P. 30(e).

§ 12.3 Waiver

These rights, however, may be waived. The deponent can waive reading, examination and signature. Fed.R.Civ.P. 30(e). Waiver can be voluntary or involuntary. If the witness fails to sign the deposition within 30 days of its submission to him for any reason whatsoever, the officer will sign for him, effectively waiving his right to signature. When the officer signs for the witness, the deposition can be used at trial as if the witness had signed unless, on a motion to suppress the record at trial, the court makes the unlikely ruling that the reasons for the refusal to sign justify excluding the record from evidence. Fed.R.Civ.P. 30(e).

More often, however, the deponent's right to read, change and sign the deposition is expressly waived by counsel. At some point in the deposition, the officer before whom the examination is taken or the opposing counsel will ask the defending attorney whether "signature is waived." Because the question may come at the end of the examination when the deposition atmosphere is more relaxed or may come as part of a series of questions regarding "usual" stipulations, defending attorneys frequently waive signature without giving it much thought.

Although signature can be expressly or constructively waived, a defending attorney should *never* waive signature. The deponent has absolutely nothing to gain, and everything to lose by waiving signature. The waiver of signature prevents the deponent and counsel from examining the deposition record. More importantly, such waiver precludes the witness from making any changes to that record. Hence, glaring and harmful errors in the transcription of deposition testimony will go uncorrected. And damaging testimony which might have for good reason been softened or modified by changes before signing will stand.

The defending attorney, therefore, must ensure that signature is not waived. First, the attorney must never expressly state that signature is waived. This seems easy. But in the midst of a deposition, it requires careful attention to the officer's "usual stipulations" and to opposing counsel's efforts to secure waiver of signature by framing the issue as part of a series of waiver questions regarding deposition routine.

Second, because the rule allows *party* deponents to waive signature, the defending attorney should make sure that the witness does not indicate any desire to waive signature. It is not uncommon for deponents to vent their frustration with the entire deposition process by casually stating that they never want to see a record of the deposition as long as they live. That kind of off-the-cuff comment should be avoided. Before the deposition begins, the defending attorney should explain to the deponent his right to sign the deposition and instruct him not to waive that right.

Third, the defending attorney must guard against constructive waiver. The witness has only 30 days from the date the record is submitted to him to make changes prior to signature. The failure to sign the deposition within 30 days will be construed as a waiver of signature. The rules require the officer to sign for the witness after 30 days even if the witness is ill or unavailable.

Presumably, the witness can obtain an enlargement of time. If, however, the witness needs more time in which to examine the record before signing, the defending attorney should not only seek an agreement from opposing counsel, but should also obtain an agreement from the officer.

Fourth, in the unfortunate circumstance in which signature has been constructively waived, the defending attorney may seek an order excluding the deposition record from trial due to errors in its transcription. *See* Fed.R.Civ.P. 32(d)(4).

§ 12.4　Changes in Deposition Testimony

The preservation of signature allows the deponent to make changes in the deposition testimony. In deciding whether to advise those changes, the defending attorney must understand the scope of changes, their use at trial and the proper formalities. Forms 12–3 thru 12–6 guide the attorney in making the decision whether to change testimony.

§ 12.5　The Scope of Changes

The deponent may make changes in the "form or substance" of deposition testimony. Fed. R.Civ.P. 30(e). The changes can be made even if they completely contradict the original answers. Allen & Co. v. Occidental Petroleum Corp., 49 F.R.D. 337 (S.D.N.Y.1970). The changes in fact may be made for any reason at all. *See* Sanford v. CBS, Inc., 594 F.Supp. 713, 715 (N.D.Ill.1984). In reviewing the deposition testimony, therefore, the defending attorney and the deponent should not only look for inadvertent errors in transcription. Rather, the *substance* of the testimony must be thoroughly reviewed to determine whether it should be changed.

§ 12.6 Use of Changes at Trial

Although the rules permit any substantive changes which the deponent in private consultation with counsel desires, those changes can have adverse consequences. If the changes have rendered the original deposition incomplete or useless, the examiner will be able to re-open the examination at the deponent's expense. The changes can also backfire at trial. Before making a substantive change, the defending attorney must understand the trial risks involved. The opposing counsel will be able to use *both* the original deposition answers and the changes at trial. In addition, opposing counsel will be granted wide latitude in cross-examining the deponent at trial regarding the reasons for the changes and the process by which they were made. Thus, unless the changes have been made for good reason, the deponent will be easily, and unnecessarily, impeached at trial.

§ 12.7 Formalities

Although courts do not scrutinize the substance of deposition changes, they do scrutinize the procedures used to make them. After deciding to make changes, the defending attorney must:

1. Retain the original deposition answers;
2. Submit the original testimony together with the changes to the officer, who will formally place them on the record;
3. Enter the changes on the deposition record itself rather than on a separate sheet, unless the deposition was not recorded stenographically;
4. Submit to the officer a statement containing the specific reasons for each and every change, rather than a conclusory statement at the end of the record.

See e.g. Lugtig v. Thomas, 89 F.R.D. 639 (N.D.Ill.1981). Changes which do not comport with these procedures will be amended or even stricken.

§ 12.8 The Decision to Change Testimony

The decision to change testimony requires a balance of the harm created at trial by the original testimony with the harm created at trial by the fact that the testimony has been changed. Because both the original damaging testimony and the change are read at trial, the change often exacerbates the original damage by permitting the jury to add the insult of impeachment to the injury of substantive testimony.

As a general rule, therefore, changes in deposition testimony should not be made unless the defending attorney can "sell" the reasons for the changes to a jury. A jury will certainly see that changes due to clerical errors are justified and thus such changes should always be made. But where substantive changes are made, the reasons better be good. The following is an non-exhaustive list of reasons for changing deposition testimony which may justify the changes to a jury:

(1) The witness did not understand the question.

(2) The witness, acting in accordance with his duty to supplement discovery responses pursuant to Federal Rule of Civil Procedure 26(e)(2)(A), has obtained information upon the basis of which he knows that his original response was incorrect when made; or

(3) The witness, acting in accordance with his *duty* to supplement discovery responses pursuant to Federal Rule of Civil Procedure 26(e)(2)(B), knows that his original response, though correct when made, is no longer true.

§ 12.9 Certification and Filing

The process of certifying and filing the deposition is the primary responsibility of the examining attorney and the officer. Nonetheless, because the defending attorney may wish to use parts of the deposition at trial or in pre-trial motions, he should ensure that these formal requirements have been satisfied.

First, the defending attorney should request a copy of the deposition from the officer. If the copy is needed on an expedited basis, the defending attorney should not rely upon opposing counsel to provide copies. Instead, the attorney should bear the added expense of securing an expedited copy from the officer.

Second, the defending party should make sure that the officer has certified the oath, the accuracy of the deposition record and any changes made on that record. Fed.R.Civ.P. 30(f).

Third, the defending party should ensure that documents marked for identification during the deposition are annexed to the record. But if those documents were produced by the deponent, the defending attorney should retain the originals.

Fourth, the defending attorney should ensure that the deposition has been properly filed, where filing is required.

Fifth, the defending attorney whose deponent offered testimony under a protective order securing its confidentiality must also make certain that the officer has sealed the deposition in an envelope marked, "Filed Under Seal," "Confidential" or some other indicia of confidentiality.

Form 12–1

Defending Party's Deposition Summary

Attention Mark	Substantive Notes
to follow up	
to probe	
to clarify	
to reconsider later after other information is gathered	

Form 12-2

Defending Party's Post-Deposition Checklist

Deponent: _____

_____   Deponent's signature

_____   Signature Expressly Waived

_____   Signature Waived by Lapse of 30 Days

_____   Signature Waived by Unavailability of Deponent

_____   Changes Made Correctly

_____   Changes Made in Margin Next to Original Answers

_____   Original Answers Retained

_____   Reasons Given For Changes Made

_____   Reasons Provided for each Change

_____   Reasons Adequate

_____   Changes Challenged

_____   Changes Used at Trial

Form 12-3

Catalogue of Changes

Deponent: _____

Questions	Tr. Pg.	Original Answer	Tr. Pg.	Change	Reason	Notes on Case at Trial

Form 12–4

Scrutiny of Changes

Deponent: _____

Original	Change	Tr. Pg.	Procedural Adequacy				Reasons Adequate	Judicial Relief Necessary
			Signature Reserved	Changes Made in 30 Days	Original Retained	Reasons Given		

Form 12–5

Deposing Party's Potential Response to Changes

Deponent: _____

1. Motion to strike change, if

    (a) Signature waived, by

        1. Express statement on record at deposition.

        2. Lapse of 30 days.

        3. Unavailability of Deponent.

    (b) Original answers not retained.

    (c) Changes do not accompany original answers.

    (d) No reasons given for changes.

2. Motions to re-open examination, if

    (a) Changes render original examination useless, or

    (b) Changes render original examination incomplete.

3. Use of change at trial

    (a) Impeachment as with any change.

    (b) Cross-examination of reasons for change.

    (c) Cross-examination as to persons who formulated the changes.

Form 12–6

Use of Changes at Trial

Deponent: _____

Original	Tr. Pg.	Change	Reason	Impeachment/Cross-Examination	Notes

Part IV

USE OF DEPOSITION AT TRIAL

Chapter 13

PREPARING THE DEPOSITION FOR USE AT TRIAL

Table of Sections

---

§ 13.1 Introduction

The deposition serves two primary, and sometimes conflicting, goals: (1) under the "pyramid" approach to discovery, where the deposition is the ultimate fact-gathering device, it is used as a vehicle for discovering further evidence; (2) under the "contention" approach to discovery, where the deposition is part of a process of eliminating contested issues between adversaries, it can produce evidence for trial.

If the deposition is used as part of a "contention" approach to discovery, the examiner takes that deposition with an eye toward using it at trial. For that examiner, the possible uses of the deposition at trial are an integral part of the deposition itself. He must understand how the deposition record can be used at trial even before he takes the deposition.

But some depositions will never be used at trial. Of course, the case may settle after discovery, but before trial. Further, under the "pyramid" approach to discovery, the deposition is merely a vehicle for further discovery and not intended ever to be introduced into evidence at trial. Indeed, in some jurisdictions, (*see* Appendix A), the examiner must designate in advance of the deposition that it is an "evidence" deposition in order to use the testimony fully at trial. Where the examiner does not intend to use the deposition at trial or has designated the deposition a "discovery deposition," he will tend to pay little attention to the potential trial uses of that deposition.

That is a mistake. For even the examiner who has no intention of using the deposition at trial must consider its possible trial uses. Before the examiner can decide whether the testimony should be used at trial, he must understand how the testimony can be used at trial. He should at least convey to his adversary the impression that the testimony will be used at trial. Further, because as every seasoned trial lawyer knows, the value of certain testimony increases or decreases throughout the litigation, the examiner should take a deposition with the thought that the testimony may have to be used at trial. Depositions are typically a one-time shot at a key witness. The examiner cannot count on being able to reopen a deposition to obtain trial testimony missed the first time. Accordingly, even examining attorneys who firmly believe that the deposition will never be used at trial must understand its potential trial uses and must take the deposition in light of those uses. Form 13–1, the trial preparation checklist, should thus be used both before the deposition and in preparing the deposition for trial.

§ 13.2 Designating Deposition Testimony

Federal courts and most state courts have the authority to order the parties to agree in advance of trial as to how significant aspects of that trial will be conducted. *See e.g.,* Fed.R. Civ.P. 16. In addition, those courts may exercise "reasonable control" over the mode of presenting evidence so as to ensure that "truth" is ascertained in an efficient manner. *See e.g.,* Fed.R.Evid. 611(a). As part of their power to conduct the presentation of evidence at trial, courts typically require the adversaries to complete a pre-trial order. This pre-trial order includes statements by each party regarding the witnesses they expect to call at trial and the documents they expect to introduce. Furthermore, the pre-trial order routinely requires each party to designate those depositions and deposition transcript pages they expect to read into evidence at trial. The examiner's first task, therefore, in preparing to use a deposition at trial will likely be to decide which deposition parts should be used at trial and then to designate those parts on the pre-trial order.

§ 13.3 Selecting Deposition Testimony to Designate

In deciding which deposition testimony to designate for trial, the lawyer must rely on his own trial strategy in light of the nature of the case. Beyond strategy and instinct, however, the lawyer should keep the following points in mind in designating deposition testimony:

(1) As a general rule, rebuttal testimony need not be designated in advance of trial. Thus, designations should be limited to testimony needed to prove or refute the case-in-chief.

(2) On the other hand, testimony designated need not be used at trial. The designator, therefore, should err on the side of designating too much rather than too little. Within the bounds of good faith, the designator should follow the maxim: when in doubt, designate!

(3) The material designated must be admissible in evidence. Thus, the designator should ensure that aspects of testimony necessary to lay the foundation for additional testimony are included in the designations.

(4) If the party intends to use at trial a videotaped deposition, the designation process involves editing and counter-editing the videotape. Thus, the designation process should begin well in advance of trial.

(5) As discussed in § 13.4, the designator should remember that the adversary has the right to read into evidence parts of the deposition testimony which in fairness ought to be read at the same time as the designator's parts. Accordingly, the designator may wish to include as part of his designations unfavorable material so as not to allow the adversary to highlight that material as part of an argument at trial on the "completeness" of the deposition testimony.

§ 13.4 Formally Designating the Testimony

The actual designation of deposition testimony involves the physical act of marking the deposition transcript to indicate which portions will be read at trial and listing the transcript pages in a pre-trial order. The designation process is one of give and take between the parties.

The party intending to use deposition testimony first designates that testimony. The adversary then affirmatively designates other portions which it intends to use. The parties also designate portions which in "fairness" ought to be read at the same time as the adversary's designations and portions which will be read after the adversary's designations of each witness as cross-examination. The original designator, of course, also has the right to counter and cross-designate his adversary's testimony.

To simplify this process, the parties should agree on a method of marking the testimony. Typically, each party will adopt a particular color of highlighter and then bracket or highlight the testimony they intend to read with that color. Moreover, each party will select other colors to be used for their counter-designations and cross-designations. Form 13–2 is a designation color chart.

In cases where many depositions will be read at trial, the parties should, in addition to designating testimony, also mark their preserved objections to the adversary's designations. The objections, or abbreviations of the objections, should be marked on the transcript in the margin next to the alleged objectionable testimony. This pre-trial designation and objection process enables the judge to rule in advance on many objections, saving precious court time. Where, however, objectionable testimony could have been cured if objected to at deposition, the failure to object constitutes a waiver of the objection. Thus, in designating testimony, the designator should review the transcript to determine the adversary's right to object to that testimony. But the designator need not and should not include in the designation his adversary's objection or other extraneous colloquy between counsel. Forms 13–3 thru 13–6 provide a method of organizing the various designations and any objections to them.

§ 13.5 Selecting a Method of Presentation

Nothing can be more boring and thus ineffectual than reading to a jury pages upon pages of deposition testimony. Where possible, and compatible with trial strategy, deposition testimony should be avoided in favor of live witnesses. Yet, depositions are often the only available source of needed testimony. The lawyer's challenge is to present that testimony in a clear, quick and compelling manner. Form 13–7 provides a worksheet for the order of live and deposition witnesses at trial.

Within the contours of each case, the following guidelines should be followed:

(1) Vary the use of deposition and live testimony.

(2) Use videotaped depositions where appropriate.

(3) Read into the record only that deposition testimony which is absolutely necessary for the case, and

(4) Do not begin or conclude a trial presentation with deposition testimony.

§ 13.6 Recreating the Deposition Atmosphere

When actually presenting the deposition testimony at trial, attorneys should endeavor to recreate the atmosphere of the deposition. Too often, attorneys simply use members of their "trial team" to read the testimony into the record. This approach should be avoided. Attorneys are bad actors and actresses. Their partisan efforts to read testimony with various inflections appears silly to jurors. And the presence of trial attorneys in different "roles" can also be awkward and confusing to a jury. At best, this method of presentation will be dry.

Instead, attorneys should employ professional actors or members of their firm who are not on the trial team as deposition readers. In this way, the trial attorney can maintain his posture as examiner, while the actor "becomes" the witness for the jury. With adequate preparation, the actor can be coached to read the transcript with the desired inflections. The actor or actors also represent fresh faces to the jurors, keeping them relatively alert during the reading.

§ 13.7   Minimizing Awkwardness With a Cautionary Instruction

The process of deposition reading not only becomes boring, but at times even absurd. When, for example, an attorney reads his adversary's deposition questions as part of his trial presentation, he assumes the adversary's persona for those questions. This process is particularly confusing when the adversary reads a question at trial to which *he* objected at the time of the deposition. Few people in the courtroom will be able to sort out the question, the answer and the objection. Does a party waive an objection to the form of a question which his adversary is reading at trial, but which he asked at the deposition? Such questions become routine (and routinely unanswerable) in complex litigation.

The best that the designating attorney and the judge can do to minimize this awkward process is to issue a cautionary instruction to the jury. Thus a party wishing to designate deposition testimony to be read at trial should seek the following preliminary instruction:

> Depositions may be received in evidence in this case. Depositions contain sworn testimony, with counsel for each party being entitled to ask questions. Testimony produced in a deposition may be read to you in open court or may be played for you on a television set or from a videotape player. Deposition testimony may be accepted by you, subject to the same instructions which apply to witnesses testifying in open court.

> In considering the deposition testimony, however, you should remember that the lawyer who reads or uses the testimony at trial may not have been the lawyer who asked the questions at the time the deposition was taken. In addition, the person who reads deposition testimony at trial may not be the person who actually gave that testimony. Accordingly, in considering the testimony, you may not consider the question or any assertions contained in the question as evidence. Rather, only the witness' answers to the questions are to be considered as evidence in this case.

See e.g. Devitt, Blackmar & Wolf, Federal Jury Practice and Instructions, §§ 70.03, 71.12.

§ 13.8   Preparation for Fairness and Cross–Designations

After the attorney has designated those deposition portions which he wishes to read into evidence at trial, the adversary has the right to designate those portions which in "fairness" ought to be read at the same time as the original designations and those portions which ought to be read after each witness's designations are completed as cross-examination.

§ 13.9   Fairness Designations

Federal Rule of Evidence 106 and its state equivalents provide that when a "recorded statement or part thereof is introduced by a party, an adverse party may require the introduction at that time of any other part or any other writing or recorded statement which at that time ought in fairness to be considered contemporaneously with it."

Federal Rule of Civil Procedure 32(a)(4) repeats this rule of evidence with specific regard to depositions:

> If only part of a deposition is offered in evidence by a party, an adverse party may require the offeror to introduce any other part which ought in fairness to be considered with the part introduced, and any party may introduce any other parts.

Although this civil discovery rule does not expressly give the adversary the right to introduce "other" deposition parts at the same time the initial parts are introduced, the evidence rule does require contemporaneous introduction, and the courts have construed the two provisions *in pari materia. See e.g.* Westinghouse Elec. Corp. v. Wray Equipment Corp., 286 F.2d 491, 494 (1st Cir.1961).

The designator should realize, therefore, that the adversary will be allowed to read into evidence additional deposition testimony which the court believes should be read out of "fairness" at the time the designator's testimony is read. By this procedure, the adversary can interrupt the flow of the designator's own case, highlight damaging testimony and cast doubt on the designator's forthrightness before the jury. The best way for the designator to prevent this embarrassing interruption is to ensure the completeness of the original designations. Alternatively, the designator should be prepared to argue the limited scope of fairness designations.

The purposes of fairness designations limit their scope. They rest upon the evidentiary principle of "completeness." The Advisory Committee Notes to Federal Rule of Evidence 106 explain that fairness designations are designed to prevent the misleading impression created from taking a statement out of context, by placing the statement back in its context at a point in the proceedings close enough in time to the original statement so as to correct the misimpression.

The trial court is granted wide discretion to ensure that the presentation of one party's case through deposition testimony is not encumbered by lengthy readings from the adversary. Fairness requires that the adversary be allowed to designate only those parts of deposition testimony which are necessary to correct any misimpression created by taking the original designations out of their context. The designator can prevent the adversary's use of fairness designations, therefore, by simply avoiding the temptation to wrench valuable testimony out of context.

§ 13.10 Cross–Designations

The designator can also minimize the impact of fairness designations by understanding and arguing the difference between such designations and cross-designations. Fairness designations are portions of testimony which are necessary to cure misimpressions created when the original designations are taken out of context. Cross-designations, on the other hand, are portions of deposition testimony which the adversary chooses to read to impeach or contradict the originally designated testimony. Cross-designations are subject to the rules governing any cross-examination at trial. Hence, the scope of cross-designations is limited to the subject matter of the direct examination. *See e.g.* Fed.R.Evid. 611(b). Moreover, the admissibility of cross-designations which go beyond those needed for completeness is governed by the traditional rules of evidence.

The distinction between fairness designations and cross-designations is important to the timing of the testimony. If the court finds that the deposition portions ought in "fairness" be read with the initial designations, then those portions must be read contemporaneously with the initial portions. If, however, the court finds that the portions are beyond the scope of fairness designations and are instead properly read as cross-examination, then those portions are not read until after all of the initial designations for a witness are completed.

Finally, if the designations are not only beyond the scope of "fairness," but also beyond the subject matter of the initial designations, then they must be read as part of the adversary's own case. This final scenario is of course the best one for the designator. Thus, in designating deposition testimony, the designator should, (1) not take testimony out of context, obviating the need for fairness designations, and (2) then be prepared to argue that the adversary's designations must be read either as part of cross-examination or—better still—as part of the adversary's own case.

Trial Preparation Checklist

Deponent _____   Date of Deposition _____

_____ Designations Completed

_____ Adversary's Fairness Designations Received

_____ Adversary's Cross–Designations Received

_____ Adversary's Affirmative Designations Received

_____ Fairness Designations to Adversary's Affirmative Designations Completed

_____ Cross–Designations to Adversary's Affirmative Designations Completed

_____ Objections to Adversary's Designations Completed

_____ Adversary's Objections to Designations Received

Form 13–2

Designation Color Chart

Deponent _____   Date of Deposition _____

Designation	Color
Deposing Party's Affirmative Designations	
Adversary's Affirmative Designations	
Deposing Party's Fairness Designations	
Deposing Party's Cross–Designations	
Adversary's Cross–Designations	
Other	

Affirmative Designations for Pre-trial Order

Deponent: _____

[*Party*] hereby designates the following portions of the deposition of [*Deponent*] which it expects to read into evidence at trial:

Transcript Page	Line to Line

Form 13–4

Fairness Designations Worksheet for Pre-trial Order

Deponent: _____

Affirmative Designations		Adversary's Fairness Doctrine		Objections possible because fairness designations not necessary to correct misimpression created by taking affirmative designation out of context
Tr. Pg.	Line to Line	Tr. Pg.	Line to Line	

Form 13–5

Cross–Designation Worksheet for Pre-trial Order

Deponent: _____

Affirmative Designation		Cross–Designation		Objections possible because beyond scope of subject matters of affirmative designation
Tr. Pg.	Line to Line	Tr. Pg.	Line to Line	

Form 13–6

Catalogue of Objections to Designations

Deponent: _____

Designations Tr. Pg.	Line to Line	Objection	Response

Form 13–7

Order of Live and Deposition Witnesses

Witness	Will Establish	Live	Deposition	Estimated Time
1.				
2.				
3.				
4.				
5.				
6.				

Form 13–8

Presentation of Deposition at Trial

Deposition	Reader for Examiner	Reader for Deponent

Chapter 14

USING THE DEPOSITION AT TRIAL

Table of Sections

§ 14.1 Introduction

The distinction between depositions used for discovery and those used for evidence at trial becomes acute when the examiner begins contemplating the introduction of deposition testimony into evidence. The scope of discovery is expressly broader than the scope of admissible testimony. Deposition questions need be only reasonably calculated to lead to admissible evidence; they need not produce admissible evidence. An answer helpful in discovery may well be inadmissible in evidence at trial. In order to avoid producing a deposition transcript which is unuseable at trial, the examiner should of course read this and the preceding chapter before even taking the deposition. Then, in preparing to use deposition testimony at trial, the examiner should return to this chapter and to Forms 14–1 thru 14–8 with the singular goal of extracting admissible evidence.

§ 14.2 Rules Governing the Use of Depositions at Trial

The rules of procedure and of evidence both govern the admissibility at trial of deposition testimony. Federal Rule of Civil Procedure 32(a) allows the use at trial of any part of a deposition against any party who received reasonable notice of the deposition. Objections to notice are waived either by attendance of the party or its representative at the deposition (Fed. R.Civ.P. 32(a)), or by failure to serve prompt written objection to the notice upon the party providing the notice. Fed.R.Civ.P. 32(d)(1).

The discovery rules, however, limit the general purposes for which a deposition can be used. The deposition of a party or an unavailable witness can be used for "any purpose." Fed.R.Civ.P. 32(a)(2), (3). But the deposition of an available, non-party witness can only be used, (1) to contradict the witness's trial testimony, (2) to impeach the witness, or (3) for any other purposes permitted by the federal rules of evidence. Fed.R.Civ.P. 32(a)(1). These discovery rules must be satisfied before a deposition can be used at trial.

Even if those discovery rules are satisfied, however, the introducing party must overcome a second obstacle. Each question and answer of deposition testimony must also be admissible under the rules of evidence, which are applied as if the deponent were testifying live at trial. Deposition testimony, therefore, can be used at trial only if the rules of procedure and of evidence are both satisfied.

§ 14.3 Use of Adverse Party's Deposition at Trial

The deposition of an adverse party can be used at trial for "any purpose." Fed.R.Civ.P. 32(a)(2). Included within the definition of adverse "party" are:

(1) officer of a party at the time of the deposition;

(2) director of a party at the time of the deposition;

(3) managing agent of a party at the time of the deposition; and

(4) any person designated by an organizational party to testify on its behalf.

Although some courts have stretched this rule to include within the definition of "adverse party" all deponents whose interests are "adverse" to the offeror, see e.g. Coughlin v. Capitol Cement Co., 571 F.2d 290, 308 (5th Cir.1978) (applying "any purpose" standard to available, non-party whom the court presumed to be adverse to offeror), the rule is limited to deponents who are *both* parties and adverse to the offering party. There is no doubt, however, that the deposition of an individual who qualifies as an adverse party can, under the discovery rules, be used for any purpose, even when the deponent is available to testify at trial. *See e.g.,* Fey v. Walston & Co., Inc., 493 F.2d 1036 (7th Cir.1974). The deposing party, using Form 14–2, can plan to use the deposition of such an adverse party, therefore, at trial for any purpose, including as substantive evidence. However, the offering party must also be certain that each portion of the testimony be admissible under the rules of evidence as if the deponent's testimony were being given live.

§ 14.4 Use of Unavailable Witness's Deposition at Trial

The deposition of a party or a non-party who is unavailable at trial may also be used at trial for "any purpose," including as substantive evidence. *See e.g.* Fed.R.Civ.P. 32(a)(3); Form 14–3. The unavailability of the witness is determined by the court as of the time the testimony is offered at trial. *See e.g.* United States v. IBM Corp., 90 F.R.D. 377 (S.D.N.Y.1981). A witness is unavailable within the meaning of the rule if the court finds that at the time his testimony is offered at trial, he is:

(1) Dead.

(2)(a) More than 100 miles from the place of trial, measured as-the-crow-flies, *see e.g.* SCM Corp. v. Xerox Corp., 76 F.R.D. 214 (D.Conn.1977), and in accordance with judicial notice. Ikerd v. Lapworth, 435 F.2d 197 (7th Cir.1970), or

　　　(b) outside of the United States.

If, however, the witness's absence was affirmatively caused by the offering party, the deposition will not be admissible as substantive evidence.

(3) Unable to attend or testify because of age, illness, infirmity of imprisonment, or

(4) Unable to be compelled to testify by subpoena.

In addition, regardless of the unavailability of the deponent under these rules, the court has authority to allow the deposition to be used where the offering party has, with proper notice, moved and shown that "exceptional circumstances" exist which make it desirable to introduce the deposition itself into evidence. Fed.R.Civ.P. 32(a)(3).

In ruling on the motion to allow such deposition testimony, however, the court must give due regard to the policy of presenting live, oral testimony in court wherever possible. *Id.* While rare, rulings that "exceptional circumstances" exist can arise where the necessity of a witness's testimony becomes apparent to counsel in the middle of trial and the court decides not to grant a continuance to allow the procurement of the witness. *See e.g.* Huff v. Marine Tank Testing Corp., 631 F.2d 1140 (4th Cir.1980). Thus, where the court finds exceptional circumstances or where the deponent is otherwise unavailable to provide live testimony, a deposition can be used for "any purpose," provided that the testimony is admissible under the rules of evidence.

§ 14.5 Use of Available, Non-party Depositions at Trial

Federal Rule of Civil Procedure 32(a)(1), in keeping with the policy favoring the presentation of live testimony at trial, limits the use of the deposition testimony of non-parties who are available at trial:

> Any deposition may be used by any party for the purpose of contradicting or impeaching the testimony of deponent as a witness, or for any other purpose permitted by the Federal Rules of Evidence.

When the deposition is used to contradict testimony or to impeach a witness, it is not admitted as substantive evidence. Rather, the deposition transcript of a deponent can be used merely to attack the testimony or credibility of that deponent when he offers live testimony at trial. Inconsistencies within the deposition itself thus cannot be used to "impeach" the deponent unless the deponent testifies at trial. *See* Rogers v. Roth, 477 F.2d 1154 (10th Cir. 1973).

The deposition of an available, non-party witness may also be used for any purpose permitted by the federal rules of evidence. Those rules expand the possible uses for deposition testimony by permitting:

(1) The use of a deposition to impeach one's own witness, where the witness offers live testimony, Fed.R.Evid. 607;

(2) The use of a deposition to refresh a live witness' recollection. Fed.R.Evid. 612, 803(5); and

(3) The use of a deposition as a prior statement of the witness which need not be shown to the witness. Fed.R.Evid. 613(a).

More significantly, however, the federal rules of evidence allow use of an available, non-party deposition as *substantive evidence* where:

(1) The deposition testimony is inconsistent with the deponent's live testimony, or is consistent with the deponent's live testimony but is offered to refute an allegation of inconsistency, Fed.R.Evid. 801(1);

(2) The deposition testimony is a statement by any employee of a party (not just an officer, director, managing agent or designated representative) and is offered as an admission of a party opponent. Fed.R.Evid. 801(d)(2); or

(3) The deposition testimony has sufficient "circumstantial guarantees of trustworthiness" so as to allow its introduction into evidence. Fed.R.Civ.P. 803(24).

Form 14–4 sets forth these various uses at trial of the depositions of an available, non-party witness.

§ 14.6 Party's Use of His Own Deposition

A party may use his own deposition at trial to contradict or impeach his own trial testimony, as permitted under the federal rules of evidence. *See* Fed.R.Evid. 607; Form 14–5. In addition, a party may introduce into substantive evidence his prior deposition testimony where that testimony is offered to rebut a claim that his trial testimony is the product of recent fabrication or improper influence or motive. Fed.R.Evid. 801(1)(B).

Otherwise, however, a party may use his own deposition at trial as substantive evidence only if he is "unavailable." In this context, "unavailability" is narrowly defined. If the party is dead or infirm at the time of the deposition, courts allow the introduction into evidence of a prior deposition. *See e.g.* Treharne v. Callahan, 426 F.2d 58 (3d Cir.1970). Moreover, the majority rule allows a party who at the time of trial is more than 100 miles from the courthouse to introduce his own deposition into evidence. *See* Richmond v. Brooks, 227 F.2d 490 (2d Cir.1955). Although this rule permits a party to "procure" his own unavailability, the courts have reasoned that because the rule makes no distinction between parties and non-parties (Fed.R.Civ.P. 32(a)(3)), parties are free to choose not to appear live at trial if they choose. *Id.*

§ 14.7 Use of Deposition From Prior Action

Depositions taken in federal or state court actions can be used in subsequent federal actions under limited circumstances. First, the original deposition must have been properly filed. Second, the deposition must have been lawfully taken, under the rules governing the jurisdiction in which the original action was filed. Third, the subsequent federal action must involve the same "subject matter" as the original action. Fourth, the subsequent action must involve the same parties as the original action, or at least their representatives or successors in interest. Fed.R.Civ.P. 32(a)(4). *See also* Form 14–6. The deposition can be used even if the action in which it was taken has not been dismissed.

The federal discovery rules, however, also permit the use of prior depositions in any other manner sanctioned by the federal rules of evidence. Under those rules, if the deponent is unavailable to testify in the current proceeding, his prior deposition testimony can be introduced into evidence if that testimony was lawfully taken and if the party against whom that testimony is currently being offered (or a predecessor in interest) had a full and fair opportunity to examine the deponent. Fed.R.Evid. 804(b)(1). The party currently offering the examination into evidence need not have been a party to the initial proceedings. Nor, under the rules of evidence, need the subject matters of the two actions be similar, so long as the party against whom the deposition is currently offered had a fair opportunity to examine the deponent.

§ 14.8 Limits on the Use of Depositions at Trial Under the Rules of Evidence

A deposition cannot be used at trial for any purpose unless the portions offered are "admissible under the rules of evidence applied as though the witness were there and testifying." Fed.R.Civ.P. 32(a). Hence, the offering party must ensure that:

(1) the testimony is relevant, Fed.R.Evid. 401;

(2) the testimony's probative value outweighs its prejudicial impact, Fed.R.Evid. 403;

(3) the testimony is not redundant, cumulative, confusing or a waste of time, Fed.R.Evid. 403;

(4) the testimony is a proper method of establishing character, where appropriate, Fed.R. Evid. 404;

(5) the testimony does not run afoul of any exclusion based on public policy, such as subsequent remedial measures, Fed.R.Evid. 407–412;

(6) the testimony is not subject to any available privilege, Fed.R.Evid. 501;

(7) the witness is competent to testify as to the offered matters, Fed.R.Evid. 601–607, 701–706;

(8) the method of interrogation (*i.e.* leading questions) was proper, Fed.R.Evid. 611; and

(9) the testimony is not otherwise inadmissible as hearsay. Fed.R.Evid. 801–805.

In addition, the party designating the deposition transcript must remember the rule of "completeness." Portions of deposition testimony will be admitted only in their proper context. Deposition testimony, therefore, must be offered together with all portions necessary to correct any misimpression created by reading that testimony out of context. Fed.R.Civ.P. 32(d)(4).

Form 14–7 provides a checklist of the possible evidentiary objections.

§ 14.9 Objections to Admissibility of Deposition Testimony at Trial

Any objection to the admissibility of deposition testimony not waived may be made at trial. Fed.R.Civ.P. 32(b). Objections to deposition notice, to the qualifications of the officer, to the oath, to the completion of the deposition record and to the form of written deposition questions are waived if they are not made promptly. *See* Fed.R.Civ.P. 32(d)(1), (2), (3), (4).

More importantly, objections as to the admissibility of evidence at trial can be waived if the objection goes to the form of the deposition question or if the basis for the objection could have been removed if it had been raised at the deposition. Fed.R.Civ.P. 32(d)(3)(A). As a general rule, these objections do not involve the substance of the testimony. In fact, the rules create a presumption that objections to the competency of the witness and the relevance of the testimony are not waived by the failure to make them at deposition. Fed.R.Civ.P. 32(d)(3)(A). The presumption is rebutted only upon a difficult showing that such objections could have been cured if raised at deposition. Form 14–8 is a worksheet which enables the attorney to organize the possible objections to the admissibility of deposition testimony at trial.

Form 14–1

Catalogue of Depositions Used at Trial

Deposition	Adverse Party	Unavailable Witness	Available Non-Party	Own	Taken in Prior Action

Form 14–2

Use of Adverse Party's Deposition at Trial

Deponent: _____

1. If Deponent Adverse Party at time of deposition?

   (a) Officer of Party?

   (b) Director of Party?

   (c) Managing Agent of Party?

   (d) Person designated by Party to testify on its behalf?

2. If Deponent is Adverse Party, Deposition can be used for

   (a) Any purpose,

   (b) As substantive evidence;

3. Provided, that it is not subject to a preserved evidentiary objection.

Form 14–3

Use of Unavailable Non-party Witness Deposition at Trial

Deponent: _____

1. Is non-party deponent unavailable because:

    (a) Dead?

    (b) More than 100 miles from place of trial?

    (c) Outside the United States?

    (d) Infirm or incapacitated?

    (e) Outside the reach of a subpoena?

2. If non-party deponent is unavailable, testimony can be used

    (a) For any purpose, and

    (b) As substantive evidence at trial,

    (c) Provided there is no preserved evidentiary objection.

3. If non-party deponent is available, court may nonetheless allow deposition into evidence under "exceptional circumstances."

Use of Available Non-party Deposition at Trial

Deponent: _____

A. Not as Substantive Evidence—

   1. Impeachment.

   2. Contradictory trial testimony.

   3. To impeach one's own witness.

   4. Refresh recollection.

   5. As a prior statement not shown to live witness.

B. As Substantive Evidence—

   1. Prior inconsistent statement.

   2. Prior consistent statement where consistency challenged.

   3. Admission by party opponent, even if made by low level employees.

   4. Where other "circumstantial guarantees of trustworthiness" exist.

Party's Use of His Own Deposition

A. Not as Substantive Evidence—but may be used to:
   1. Impeach own testimony
   2. Contradict own testimony

B. May be used as Substantive Evidence, if unavailable because:
   1. Dead?
   2. Infirm?, or
   3. More than 100 miles from place of trial?

Form 14–6

Use of Deposition From Prior Action

Prior Action	Subject Matter	Deposition Date	Parties Present	Current Parties	Current Parties or Surrogates Had Opportunity and Motive to Examine Originally

Form 14–7

Checklist of Evidentiary Objections

1. Relevance _____

2. Probative value outweighs prejudice _____

3. Cumulative _____

4. Improper _____

5. Testimony excluded for public policy _____

6. Competency of lay or expert witness _____

7. Proper method of interrogation _____

8. Hearsay _____

Form 14–8

Objection to Admissibility Worksheet

Questions Objected To	Objections		When Objection Made			Objection Waived	Objection Response	Admitted
	Curable	Non-curable	At Dep.	In Pre-trial	At Trial			

Appendix

DEPOSITION RULES IN EACH STATE

FEDERAL
RULE 26(b)(1)
Para. 1

(b) **Discovery Scope and Limits.** Unless otherwise limited by order of the court in accordance with these rules, the scope of discovery is as follows:—

(1) In General. Parties may obtain discovery regarding any matter, *not privileged* (emphasis added), which is relevant to the subject matter involved in the pending action, whether it relates to the claim or defense of the party seeking discovery or to the claim or defense of any other party, including the existence, description, nature, custody, condition and location of any books, documents, or other tangible things and the identity and location of persons having knowledge of any discoverable matter. It is not ground for objection that the information sought will be inadmissible at the trial if the information sought appears reasonably calculated to lead to the discovery of admissible evidence.

ALABAMA
RULE 26(b)(1)

Identical to Federal Rule 26(b)(1), Para. 1

ALASKA
RULE 26(b)(1)

Identical to Federal Rule 26(b)(1), Para. 1

ARIZONA
RULE 26(b)(1)

Identical to Federal Rule 26(b)(1), Para. 1

ARKANSAS
RULE 26(b)(1)

Substantially similar to Federal Rule 26(b)(1), Para. 1. Subsection substitutes "issues" for "subject matter involved." It omits the location of "any books, documents, or other tangible things," and instead focuses on the location of persons who have knowledge of any discoverable matter *or who will or may be called as a witness at the trial of any cause* (emphasis added).

CALIFORNIA
SECTION 2016(b)

Substantially similar to Federal Rule 26(b)(1), Para. 1. Scope of examination is subject to subdivision (b) or (d) of Section 2019 of this code. Subsection (b) has also added that, "All matters which are privileged against disclosure upon the trial under the law of this state are privileged against disclosure through any discovery procedure. This article shall not be construed to change the law of this state with respect to the existence of any privilege, whether provided for by statute or by judicial decision."

SECTION 2023(a)(1)

Misuses of the discovery process include, but are not limited to, the following: (1) Persisting, over objection and without substantial justification, in an attempt to obtain information or materials that are outside the scope of permissible discovery.

SECTION 2025(a)

Any party may obtain discovery within the scope delimited by Section 2017, and subject to the restrictions set forth in Section 2019, by taking in California the oral deposition of any person, including any party to the action.

COLORADO
RULE 26(b)(1)

Identical to Federal Rule 26(b)(1), Para. 1

CONNECTICUT SECTION 218	**Scope of Discovery—In General.** In any civil action, in any probate appeal, or in any administrative appeal where the court finds it reasonably probable that evidence outside the record will be required, a party may obtain in accordance with the provisions of this chapter discovery of information or disclosure, production and inspection of papers, books or document material to the subject matter involved in the pending action, which are *not privileged* (emphasis added), whether the discovery or disclosure relates to the claim or defense of the party seeking discovery or to the claim or defense of any other party, and which are within the knowledge, possession or power of the party or person to whom the discovery is addressed. Discovery shall be permitted if the disclosure sought would be of assistance in the prosecution or defense of the action and if it can be provided by the disclosing party or person with substantially greater facility than it could otherwise be obtained by the party seeking disclosure. It shall not be ground for objection that the information sought will be inadmissible at trial if the information sought appears reasonably calculated to lead to the discovery of admissible evidence. Written opinions of health care providers concerning evidence of medical negligence as provided by Section 12 of P.A. 86–338 shall not be subject to discovery except as provided in that section.
SECTION 219	**Scope of Discovery—Materials Prepared in Anticipation of Litigation; Statements of Parties.** A party may obtain, without the showing required under this section, discovery of his own statement and of any *nonprivileged* (emphasis added) statement of any other party concerning the action or its subject matter.
DELAWARE RULE 26(b)(1)	Identical to Federal Rule 26(b)(1), Para. 1
D.C. RULE 26(b)(1)	Identical to Federal Rule 26(b)(1), Para. 1
FLORIDA RULE 1.280(b)(1)	Identical to Federal Rule 26(b)(1), Para. 1
GEORGIA SECTION 9–11–26(b)(1)	Identical to Federal Rule 26(b)(1), Para. 1
HAWAII RULE 26(b)(1)	Identical to Federal Rule 26(b)(1), Para. 1
IDAHO RULE 26(b)(1)	Identical to Federal Rule 26(b)(1), Para. 1
RULE 26(b)(3)	. . . In ordering discovery of such materials when the required showing has been made, the court shall protect against disclosure of the mental impressions, conclusions, opinions, or legal theories of an attorney or other representative of a party concerning the litigation, *including communications between the attorney and client, whether written or oral* (emphasis added).
ILLINOIS SECTION 201(b)(2)	**Privilege and Work Product.** All matters that are privileged against disclosure on the trial, *including privileged communications between a party or his agent and the attorney for the party, are privileged against disclosure through any*

discovery procedure (emphasis added). Material prepared by or for a party in preparation for trial is subject to discovery only if it does not contain or disclose the theories, mental impressions, or litigation plans of the party's attorney. The court may apportion the cost involved in originally securing the discoverable material, including when appropriate a reasonable attorney's fee, in such manner as is just.

SECTION 219(d)	**Abuse of Discovery Procedures.** . . . If a party willfully obtains or attempts to obtain information by an improper discovery method, willfully obtains or attempts to obtain information to which he is not entitled, or otherwise abuses these discovery rules, the court may enter any order provided for in paragraph (c) of this rule.
INDIANA RULE 26(B)(1)	Identical to Federal Rule 26(b)(1), Para. 1
IOWA RULE 122(a)	Identical to Federal Rule 26(b)(1), Para. 1
KANSAS SECTION 60–226(b)(1)	Identical to Federal Rule 26(b)(1) except for addition of sentence: "Except as permitted under paragraph (3) of this subsection, a party shall not require a deponent to produce, or submit for inspection, any writing prepared by, or under the supervision of, an attorney in preparation for trial."
KENTUCKY RULE 26.02(1)	Identical to Federal Rule 26(b)(1), Para. 1
LOUISIANA ARTICLE 1422	Identical to Federal Rule 26(b)(1), Para. 1
MAINE RULE 26(b)(1)	Identical to Federal Rule 26(b)(1), Para. 1
MARYLAND RULE 2–402(a)	Substantially similar to Federal Rule 26(b)(1), Para. 1. Subsection adds that "it is not ground for objection that the information sought *is already known to or otherwise obtainable by the party seeking discovery* (emphasis added) or that the information will be inadmissible at the trial if the information sought appears reasonably calculated to lead to the discovery of admissible evidence." It also adds, "An interrogatory or deposition question otherwise proper is not objectionable merely because the response involves an opinion or contention that relates to fact or the application of law to fact."
MASSACHUSETTS RULE 26(b)(1)	Identical to Federal Rule 26(b)(1), Para. 1
MICHIGAN RULE 2.302(B)(1)(a)	Identical to Federal Rule 26(b)(1), Para. 1
RULE 2.302(B)(1)(b)	Differs from Federal Rule by adding: (b) A party who has a privilege regarding part or all of the testimony of a deponent must either assert the privilege at the deposition or lose the privilege as to that testimony for purposes of the action. A party who claims a privilege at a deposition may not at the trial offer the testimony of the deponent pertaining to the evidence objected to at the deposition.
MINNESOTA RULE 26.02(1)	Identical to Federal Rule 26(b)(1), Para. 1

MISSISSIPPI SECTION 13–1–226(b)(1)	Identical to Federal Rule 26(b)(1), Para. 1
MISSOURI RULE 56.01(b)(1)	Identical to Federal Rule 26(b)(1), Para. 1
MONTANA RULE 26(b)(1)	Identical to Federal Rule 26(b)(1), Para. 1
NEBRASKA RULE 25–1267.02	Substantially similar to Federal Rule 26(b)(1), Para. 1. When referring to persons having knowledge, "relevant" substituted for "discoverable" facts.
NEVADA RULE 26(b)(1)	Identical to Federal Rule 26(b)(1), Para. 1
NEW HAMPSHIRE RULE 35(b)(1)	Identical to Federal Rule 26(b)(1), Para. 1
RULE 44, Para. 1	The deponent, on deposition or on written interrogatory, shall ordinarily be required to answer all questions not subject to privilege or excused by the statute relating to depositions, and it is not grounds for refusal to answer a particular question that the testimony would be inadmissible at the trial if the testimony sought appears reasonably calculated to lead to the discovery of admissible evidence and does not violate any privilege.
NEW JERSEY RULE 4:10–2(a)	Substantially similar to Federal Rule 26(b)(1), Para. 1 except that subsection (a) has added "Nor is it ground for objection that the examining party has knowledge of the matters as to which discovery is sought."
NEW MEXICO RULE 1–026(B)(1)	Identical to Federal Rule 26(b)(1), Para. 1
NEW YORK SECTION 3101(b)	**Privileged Matter.** Upon objection by a party privileged matter shall not be obtainable.
NORTH CAROLINA RULE 26(b)(1)	Substantially similar to Federal Rule 26(b)(1), Para. 1 except that subsection (1) has added "Nor is it ground for objection that the examining party has knowledge of the information as to which discovery is sought."
NORTH DAKOTA RULE 26(b)(1)	Identical to Federal Rule 26(b)(1), Para. 1
OHIO RULE 26(B)(1)	Identical to Federal Rule 26(b)(1), Para. 1
OKLAHOMA SECTION 3203(B)(1)	Identical to Federal Rule 26(b)(1), Para. 1
OREGON RULE 36(B)(1)	Substantially the same as Federal Rule 26(b)(1), Para. 1 except for some different language.
PENNSYLVANIA RULE 4003.1	Substantially similar to Federal Rule 26(b)(1), Para. 1. Scope of discovery is subject to Rules 4003.2 to 4003.5 inclusive and Rule 4011.
RULE 4011(c)	**Limitation of Scope of Discovery and Deposition.** No discovery or deposition shall be permitted which relates to matter which is privileged.
RHODE ISLAND RULE 26(b)(1)	Substantially similar to Federal Rule 26(b)(1), Para. 1. Scope of examination subject to Rule 30(b) or (d).

SOUTH CAROLINA
RULE 26(b)(1)

Identical to Federal Rule 26(b)(1), Para. 1

SOUTH DAKOTA
SECTION 15–6–26(b)

Identical to Federal Rule 26(b)(1), Para. 1

TENNESSEE
RULE 26.02(1)

Identical to Federal Rule 26(b)(1), Para. 1

TEXAS
RULE 166b(3)(e)

Exemptions. The following matter(s) are not discoverable: (e) any matter protected from disclosure by privilege.

UTAH
RULE 26(b)(1)

Identical to Federal Rule 26(b)(1), Para. 1

VERMONT
RULE 26(b)(1)

Identical to Federal Rule 26(b)(1), Para. 1

VIRGINIA
RULE 4:1(b)(1)

Identical to Federal Rule 26(b)(1), Para. 1

RULE 4:1(b)(5)

Limitations on Discovery in Certain Procedures. In any proceeding (1) for separate maintenance, divorce, or annulment of marriage, (2) for the exercise of the right of eminent domain, or (3) for a writ of habeas corpus or in the nature of coram nobis: (a) the scope of discovery shall extend only to matters which are relevant to the issues in the proceeding and which are not privileged.

WASHINGTON
RULE 26(b)(1)

Identical to Federal Rule 26(b)(1), Para. 1

WEST VIRGINIA
RULE 26(b)(1)

Identical to Federal Rule 26(b)(1), Para. 1

WISCONSIN
SECTION 804.01(2)(a)

Identical to Federal Rule 26(b)(1), Para. 1

WYOMING
RULE 26(b)(1)

Identical to Federal Rule 26(b)(1), Para. 1

†